NEVER SETTLE

The Essential Guide to
Finding and Keeping Your Ideal Mate

Published by Treo Press

Book Layout and Cover Design by Custom-book-tique.com

www.trevortreoscott.com

NEVER SETTLE

*The Essential Guide to Finding
and Keeping your Ideal Mate*

TREVOR ANDREW SCOTT, Jr.

TREO PRESS

CONTENTS

INTRODUCTION

FINDING MY PURPOSE

[handwritten note in right margin: The Power of God's free will]

We cannot choose our birth parents, but we do have some control over the mate we spend the rest of our life with. Unfortunately such an important decision is often left to luck or chance. Society puts little emphasis on teaching us how to find our ideal love.

In this book series, you will discover lessons and principles that will help you navigate the complex world of love. There are some common traits among the couples who have been together over ten years. There are also some common lessons I have learned from those who are no longer married.

Although this book doesn't have all the answers, it will give you a few that you must absolutely know in order to find and keep lasting love.

If you are already in a relationship, the concepts, ideas and stories shared in this book will help you to refine and enhance the love you already have. Just because you have been with your mate for over a year doesn't mean you haven't missed some of the core principles that could magnify the love you have put your energy into building.

MY *AHA* MOMENT

I was on the phone with a friend who I had known for several years. It had been months since we had last spoken, and we were getting each other caught up on the lost time. We had once worked in the same insurance company.

I had spent ten years in the insurance industry, not only selling policies but I also expended a great deal of my time training others on the topic of personal development. Through live events, conference calls, and personal sessions, I trained over ten thousand people on how to bring a better version of themselves to the table of life. This of course would have made a positive impact on their selling and recruiting results in the insurance industry itself, as well as having marked "side" effects in their personal lives.

It had been some time since this friend of mine had been active in our company, as he had moved on to coaching and writing his first book. I was excited for him, because he seemed to be having all the fun in the world. You could really tell that his new endeavor caused him to feel more alive than ever before. He was pursuing his passion.

He told me how well he was doing, and I have to admit I was impressed with the income he was able to generate for himself. Then he told me something that would drastically alter the next few years of my adult life.

"Trevor, I help so many people now, and a lot of what I teach and talk about I learned from you."

Here is what I heard when he made that statement: "Trevor, you are qualified to do this." I just didn't know what "this" meant. I thought that—if I had had just a small influence on this guy who is now impacting hundreds of people through books, seminars, and coaching—how many people could I reach myself to effect changes in their lives?

That night I took a long look at my life and what I felt "this" could mean. I started taking inventory of my life. I wanted to find something that I could use to drastically impact the lives of many people in a positive manner. For a long time I recognized that this was part of my purpose because I've always enjoyed the testimonies of the people I've helped. However, I had no idea how I could fulfill such an important destiny.

"If he could do it, so could I."

That was the statement that continued to cross my mind. Sure I might have been more prepared than him, but it meant nothing without passion. "This" had to be something that pulled me to do it. He was a great career coach, but I wasn't passionate about helping someone land their dream job like he was; so I couldn't do what he did. I also didn't want to be one of those guys who taught people how to get rich when they weren't rich. I felt I had no voice if I couldn't back up what I was preaching. I guess that was the story I told myself.

We are all results of the stories we tell ourselves.

Many people desire a life with enough money to have options. I always dreamed of being in the position where money was no longer an issue so that I could spend my days living my life's purpose instead of trying to make a living.

Just imagine that you no longer have to work for money. Imagine being in a position financially where money would be deposited into your account daily whether you work or not. What would you do with your time?

Sure, you may say something like, "Well, Trevor, I would just sit on a beach all day." And that might be fun for the first few years, but, at some point, you might feel this pull to do more than just sit on a beach. That scenario is called "financial freedom."

Many books are sold each year teaching you how to reach your financial goals. Although I was on the right path to obtaining my goals, I still didn't feel comfortable teaching others things that I could not validate with my own massive success.

Finally it hit me. For the past seven years I had spent over ten thousand hours of my time focusing my personal development efforts on love and relationships. I had read over one hundred books looking for ways to improve my results with love since the public demise of my five-year relationship.

In that relationship, it didn't take very long for us to realize that we were both settling for each other. Two months before our wedding, she abruptly canceled it. To add to the pain and embarrassment, she made it clear that there was someone else who was a better fit for her.

I was devastated. I was heartbroken. I felt like my pride took the ultimate attack, and it was on display for hundreds of people around us. What I did next, I must admit, was completely different than what most people would have done.

I decided that I was going to somehow turn our broken relationship around—even if it killed me. I spent the next two years of that relationship studying every aspect of happiness when it came to love and relationships. During that time I began working with marriage counselors. I wanted to understand the common things among successful relationships. I wanted to learn who I had to become in order to turn around such a broken love story.

I also began interviewing two hundred married/divorced individuals. And for the finale I continued my scholastic study by reading over two hundred books. I wanted to know what caused a relationship to last for years and others to dwindle after a few months or even a few years. That is where I have realized there are many different paths to finding your ideal mate.

Even with all of my studying, that relationship ended simply because we were not each other's ideal mate. Without even trying, I realized I had taught myself some of the key ingredients to finding and keeping the right person. I later used everything I had learned and had experienced to find my ideal wife, and it worked!

Since that time several dozen people also found their perfect partner as a result of working with me. I've seen at least six people get married with my help. I have witnessed countless people who backed out of abusive relationships of all kinds. I have also seen dozens of people find success in their relationships in various ways. When I thought about where I had come from and where I was currently, it was clear that part of my purpose was to teach people the necessary principles to find and keep their ideal mate. I had done it over and over again for others but had never thought of doing it for a living until now.

If finding the perfect partner was the same as finding financial freedom, I would be well qualified. Let's just say that being married to your ideal spouse was the same thing as earning the amount of money you consider to being "rich." If this statement is true, that would mean I was one of the wealthiest people in the world.

Plenty of people are married, but very few can honestly say they are with their perfect mate. I'm rich, filthy rich, with information on how to find the perfect mate. I had now found the area of life that would allow me to help the most people and still feel fulfilled. I didn't find my wife because of luck. It was a direct result of applying all the principles I had learned over the last ten years, including when I was at my emotional low point.

If you speak to different millionaires, you will discover that they all took a different route to their success. However, there are usually a few common traits among the highly successful. Finding those traits or habits

6

and teaching them, in the context of relationships, became a strong desire for me.

I started to realize that, for some people, happiness, finding love, or acquiring financial freedom could be a seminar, a book, or even a telephone session away. Some people are one idea away from their life completely changing, but they think they are nowhere near their goals. Think about the point at which hot water becomes boiling water. At 211 degrees it is just hot water, but, when it increases one more degree to 212 degrees, it becomes boiling water. Only one degree changed everything for the water.

Think about the bubbles and the movement of boiling water versus hot water. There is a drastic difference. What an interesting concept. You are one degree away from all the money you will ever need or from the love of your life. I wish to continue to help people find that one degree of change that will affect everything.

There was one young lady in particular who had finished one of my workshops within seven weeks. What happened next in her life may seem like a miracle, but, I promise you, nothing could be further from the truth.

Within forty days of taking the workshop, she not only had met a great man but she had married him. Was it the workshop that made such an unbelievable event possible? That is very possible. Maybe some of the info in the workshop and contained in this book could be your one degree.

Let me explain how wealthy I am when it comes to love. I sit here looking at my wife saying to myself, "How did I get here?" We are days away from closing on a beautiful home, while my wife is months away from giving birth to our first son. It's been three years, and my wife and I still don't argue.

We have made it through a few challenges that would have derailed the average relationship, but not ours. It is still a joy to see her, and I couldn't imagine that another woman could have made me this happy. It is a joy for both of us to come home to each other. We enjoy setting goals together and accomplishing them together. We enjoy being lazy together and letting the day pass by like a taxicab in New York City. There is no aspect of my life with my wife that I am not grateful for.

Doesn't that sound like a "love-wealthy" couple?

Sure we have goals and visions for our lives that we have not met yet, but what successful couple doesn't? Remember there are different millionaires in the world. You have those who earn one million dollars per year and those who earn one hundred million dollars every twelve months. So let's just say we earn three million dollars per year, and we are looking to increase it to ten million. If you were to speak to my wife, she will tell you the same that this goal is shared by both of us.

So if I were to write a guide on how to get rich, or to find your ideal mate, how would it look?

How does a super rich person approach the task of showing people the monetary blueprint?

First of all, he or she would have to tell their story and the specific things they did to acquire the wealth they have. In an effort to be the bridge from the life you are living to the life you want and deserve to live, I now present you with the ten-plus years of research and learning that made me a millionaire in the area of love: the 60/40 Axiom to Finding Relationship/Love Wealth. To answer your impending question, "No, it has nothing to do with the 80/20 rule." Let me explain.

CHAPTER SUMMARY

Regardless of whether or not you find your ideal partner, you were put here for a reason. Spend some time each week searching for your true purpose in life. A huge part of your quest to find happiness in any area of your life and/or love is directly tied to your passion. When you find your passion, you are more alive, and that version of you can bring a unique kind of happiness to a relationship. What could you do freely and willingly all day long without ever getting paid for it?

True Love

Establishing Your Blueprint

I was walking into the bank to deposit a check when I saw an older gentleman on his way out of the same door I was about to enter. He was taking his good ol' time, so I decided to walk back out and hold the door for him. He had his brown dress socks pulled all the way up, and, yes, they still had the elastic in them. He had on a huge pair of glasses with a traditional "old-man hat."

"Thank you very much. I know I'm slow, but, hey, I'm ninety-five years old." He displayed a smile that was infectious.

I was shocked. Not so much by his age but by the fact that he was still taking care of his own affairs at the bank. He didn't have his child taking care of his errands; he was still truly independent. "Wow, sir, that's great! God has blessed you," I said.

"And I'm still driving too," he said, with a huge grin on his face. "Have a great day."

"You have a better one," I replied.

"I like that. I'm going to use that from now on."

When I got in the bank, I told the teller, "Wow, that guy that just left the bank is ninety-five years old and is still taking care of everything himself and still driving."

She smiled. "He has a wife who is ninety-three and has Alzheimer's. She remembers so much but doesn't remember him. They go out on dates every day, usually to the same place, and she remembers all of the employees, but not him. Just imagine how emotionally painful that could be for some people. He says that, at home, she usually just watches TV all day. Only last week he told me, 'We will be married seventy-one years this September, and I'm so happy that she is still with me.'"

Wow! I am not a punk, but the wind must have been blowing hard in the bank because my eyes almost started to fill with water. This just didn't seem real. He obviously loved her, but his joy and love for her wasn't dependent on how she felt about him. I'm not saying that is what love should be. But just think about it. Imagine finding that one person who you would actually love in sickness and in health. Are you so committed and so mentally tough that you can find the blessing in any situation, no matter how painful it may seem?

If you ask some people about true love, they would probably say it is more of a fable than something that can actually be obtained. Sure, quite a few people have found someone who causes them to want to hold hands, to take long walks in the park, to dance with, and to make love to. The challenge is that the majority of those couples rarely maintain this romantic period longer than a few months or even a few years before the relationship becomes a chore.

Others would refer to the term *true love* as something only seen in movies, soap operas, romance novels, poetry, various writings, and music. Maybe, just maybe, they might have known of one couple who found it and actually maintained it for the duration of their relationship. If they don't know one couple, they know someone who knows someone who actually found this thing called true love.

According to the United States Census Bureau, for first-time marriages, the divorce rates have skyrocketed to over 40 percent. Yet I'm sure they all went into the marriage thinking that it was forever! In school, if you got everything correct, you would be given a grade of A+. If you only get half of the questions right, you would be given an F.

Where did we go wrong? Is it cultural? Is it a case-by-case basis?

No matter where you travel in the world, for hundreds of years, the desire for romantic love has existed.

For most people, love rarely meets their expectations. There are plenty of people who still believe that someday they will find true love if they remain patient. It is almost as if these same people believe it is something that just happens around a certain age, like puberty or menopause. There are also people who have already found love, but they are in the cultivation stage of it, long after the butterflies are gone. Searching for it has left most people feeling like they are wandering aimlessly, like Dorothy in the story of *The Wizard of Oz*.

In that tale, the main character, Dorothy, gets taken away from her home and has to find her way to a city called Oz to meet a wizard who could possibly help her get home. Her journey takes her down a long path called "the yellow brick road," where she encounters a tin man, a lion, and a scarecrow, all of whom also needed to see the wizard. The tin man needed a heart, because he was entirely made of metal; therefore, he didn't feel alive. The scarecrow needed a brain, because he was made completely of hay. The lion needed courage, because he was scared of everything.

The foursome finally gets down the seemingly endless yellow brick road, and, after facing extreme challenges, they encounter the "wonderful" wizard. Once they met him, they ultimately learned two major things. The first thing they realized is that he was a fraud and couldn't give them what they were looking for.

However, the biggest lesson they learned was that they already possessed everything they needed within themselves. This would make you think that their journey down the yellow brick road to the wizard was unnecessary, but that was a major part of the story. The true lesson was hidden in their journey.

I think this is a metaphor for true love. I believe most of what you need to find is already inside you. However, I believe you do need certain people, experiences, and principles to guide you along your journey.

Consider this book your personal yellow brick road to finding true love. Every word carefully placed like each individual yellow brick. Each brick by itself means nothing. However, by strategically placing them together, it will provide the perfect guide to the life you want and deserve to live. Keep in mind that every heartbreak, disappointment, pain, and sadness are part of the reason that you will find everything you desire from love.

ENHANCE YOUR CURRENT LOVE BLUEPRINT

What does true love mean to you?

Each of us has a story or an ideal that we hold on to which describes what we believe love should be. We will discuss later where you may have gotten that story from, but there is no doubt that you have some idea in your mind of what love should look like.

Some people believe that love should consist of hard work, and others believe that true love should be easy. Some people believe love should be passionate or filled with drama; others feel that contentment and peace are a reflection of love. Usually if we are unhappy with our love life, it is because our current existence, or the way our love life is right now for us, doesn't match the story or the expectation that we have for love.

Let's say you believe that you should be married and have two kids by age thirty-seven, and you are now thirty-five and not in a relationship. Chances are you will be more stressed or unhappy with your love life, because where you actually are is not close to where you believe you should be.

On the other hand, if our current love experience looks like, or is better than, our love expectation, we find ourselves extremely happy with our love life. Depending on how close or how distant our actual experience is to our set point determines how stressed or happy we are with love.

Although there is no right or wrong story, there are some common things among happy couples, and it would be beneficial to at least investigate those commonalities.

Why?

You may discover that there are some things about your story that you want to alter or eliminate in order to navigate yourself to success.

If you find yourself unhappy with love, there are usually three options, according to best-selling author and dynamic speaker Tony Robbins.

Option One: You could blame someone or something other than yourself.

However, the major problem with that option is you will never have the power to change your life as long as you blame other people. Think about how many people do this. Sometimes people don't want to face the person in the mirror, because it takes away their excuse.

Option Two: To change our life so that it can match the ideal love story we have imagined for ourselves.

Reading this book and books like it is one way to change your current life conditions. It's as if you are doing the necessary things to deserve your love story.

Option Three: We may have to change our set point. This doesn't mean you are lowering your standards.

Sometimes we have unrealistic goals or we have certain restrictions on us, such as health challenges or time constraints.

Let's say you have a goal of running in a race later this week. If you break your leg the day before the race, there isn't enough time to heal for that event. In this case you have to change the goal or the set point.

If your love blueprint says you want to be married by thirty-two, and you are now thirty-one and single due to a recent breakup, that doesn't mean you *have* to change your goal or your love expectation. It really depends on who you are and what you believe you can do. It also depends on if you are, or can become, the type of person who can still get those results in spite of the circumstances.

Following this chapter, I will explain how I, like most happy people, had to change both my story and my life conditions in order to find what I wanted.

THE CHEMISTRY OF LOVE

Before I do that, let me offer a simple yet powerful story or explanation of what true love could mean. Romantic love is commonly associated with a feeling. When people say they love someone, it is often referring to how someone makes them feel or how they feel about someone. You have heard people say, "I love the way he/she makes me feel." The challenge with that is, feelings often change.

Think about it.

There has been a time in your life when you really loved something that you no longer adore. Most of us could not get enough of our favorite toys at some point in our childhood. I'm sure that most of us have outgrown the desire for G.I. Joe action figures and Barbie dolls. The point I'm trying to make here is that emotions or feelings will change.

So I ask the question, why would you base your definition of true love on something that can fade so easily?

I remember sitting in a seminar where a pastor named Myles Munroe gave a distinction between fact and truth. The word *fact* indicates something that will probably never change. It is something that usually cannot be rejected as incorrect. An example of a fact is: the world is round.

On the other hand, the word *truth* refers to something that is only correct depending on the circumstances at the time of the observation. "I am currently writing my book entitled *Never Settle*" is a statement that is a truth, because I am currently writing this book. Yet by the time you read this sentence, it is no longer true.

Do you see how the circumstance made that a truth, not a fact?

Most people's love story defines love as a truth and not a fact. It's something that may change depending on the circumstances or how they feel today.

How often do we spend months with someone, maybe even years, only to find out that they are round and not square?

The Earth being flat was once considered a fact because that is what people believed. However, through deep scientific research, it was later determined that the world being round is a fact and cannot be altered. Those who believed it was flat can no longer accept that belief as a fact but only as a truth.

It was based on the limited knowledge and tools we had to observe the planet as a whole. We later concluded that the Earth is in fact round. When I think of true love, I think of something that can endure the ultimate test, which is the test of time. I think of something that is worth fighting for. So why do so many people primarily associate love with that euphoric feeling, a truth, and not something of substance, a fact?

Dopamine and norepinephrine are chemicals that the brain produces which can cause someone to feel like they are in love. It helps control the pleasure and reward centers in our brain. Dopamine provokes a satisfactory response from us when it is prompted by something, like certain foods, coffee, drugs, nicotine, men, women, sex, etc.

Dopamine is the cause behind many addictions. It is related to euphoria and cravings. Norepinephrine has an effect on the heart, causing an increase in the rate of contractions, blood sugar levels, and blood pressure. So imagine meeting someone that triggers the flow of these chemicals in your brain. Of course you will only see these benefits, as you spend time being with this person, and your heart rate increases drastically.

Most of you have experienced this on some level. I know you have at least had a huge crush on someone at some point in your life. Imagine it was the same thing as your favorite alcoholic drink. Don't you remember that time when you had just a little too much to drink? Of course you weren't thinking clearly.

Maybe you never had a drink in your life, but you met someone who made you feel completely in love. You now know how it feels to have too much to drink. It's like the inebriation of love. Responsible people monitor their alcohol intake if they know they are going to be driving, because a lack of responsibility in this area has the ability to take many lives.

I believe the same thing is true with that initial "in love feeling." Since most people don't realize the effect of dopamine on their dating lives, they don't take the time to understand it and control it. Of course we know the consequences of drunk driving. Similarly how many lives have been ruined through unhealthy relationships, bad breakups, and divorce?

This may be a new concept to some, but many people have already experienced this in the past. You met that amazingly perfect girl or guy, and it seemed as if he or she could do no wrong. The prospective partner made your blood pressure rise, and all you could see was the benefits of being around him or her. Maybe this feeling went on for a few months. Maybe you lasted three winters with this person.

And then it happened. All of a sudden you started to notice all the things that he or she did wrong. Now you hate the fact that he leaves the toilet seat up. Yet a few years ago you wouldn't argue with him; you would simply put the seat down yourself.

A few months ago you thought that her laugh was a sound only duplicated by angels from heaven, but now you find it to be inappropriate. You thought his five-o'clock shadow made him look sexy, like a movie star. Now you can't stand kissing him because his beard scratches you, and you wish he would just shave his porcupine like face. Some of the same actions that you thought were cute years ago now annoy the hell out of you.

Many studies have shown that the feeling of deep passionate love starts to naturally lose its intensity over time, and the only way to keep it alive is to work to maintain it.

After working with marriage counselors I learned that somewhere between one and three years, you can see most of the chemicals disappear that cause those feelings. This is a scary thought to even entertain—the idea of your fact becoming a truth.

Most people associate a great relationship with that feeling of being madly in love with the other person. That feeling that seems to fall from the sky and is above any human definition. I have actually had several clients who would even say this is the same feeling that lets you know that the person you have met is your soul mate. Yet talk to those same people in a few years, and they might have moved on from that partner and are now dating someone else. Ask them, "What happened to your significant other? I thought you said he/she was definitely the one?" Of course their reaction is always, "No. I thought he/she was the one, but my new partner is definitely it."

If you fail to get this concept, you may constantly fall for nature's best hat trick. Mother Nature keeps both of you interested in each other just long enough to further our species and multiply. She could care less about if you find a happily ever after. According to *Why Men Want Sex and Women Need Love* authors Allan and Barbara Pease, they state humans are slow reproducers because women can only bear one child per year. So having different factors that can speed up the possibility of creating life is a must.

Most people have loving parents who taught them many lessons about life. Remember when your mother taught you how to do your own hair? Or about the time when your father taught you how to change a flat tire? Don't you ever wonder why your parents didn't tell you detailed instructions about how to successfully find love?

Maybe it's because they didn't know the answer.

It's hard to give someone directions to a place they have never been. Or maybe they just didn't know how and when to teach you. Some of our parents may have figured out this love thing by accident and can't really pinpoint the road map to getting to that amazing place. Maybe that is a blessing in disguise.

How can you become successful at anything if you have no idea what to do? Even the great basketball player Michael Jordan had all the talent in the world, but he has said publicly that it was practice and passion that put him at the top of his sport. So let's assume you have one part of the equation, since you decided to read this book.

If you are not passionate about finding true love, this book will not give it to you. This book may spark something in you that will cause you to start heading down a path to discover the passion inside you. Remember, that is only half of the two-part journey to relationship greatness.

Recall the example I gave about Michael Jordan. Practicing or creating a habit is the proper action required to give you your results. Sure, you may be saying, "Practice what?" There has to be a way of thinking to excel at anything in life. Some of this thinking is tied to your internal love story that you feel connotes true love.

You additionally have to have a winning mentality. You must somehow believe that what is possible is also possible for you. Before I started dating my future wife, I knew I would find her. I also knew exactly how to find her.

Of course I had to spend the time, energy, and money to learn which habits I would have to eliminate, limit, or increase.

Having a coach dramatically changed my perspective. Since I truly believed those specific things mentioned in the previous paragraph, it was easy to enjoy the dating process. It almost reminded me of the time my father was buying me a car in high school. He didn't go out and buy one right away. He took a few weeks to find the perfect vehicle for the perfect price. I was okay with taking the bus or bumming a ride from my friends because I knew a car was on the way.

This book will give you some of the key principles needed to find and keep the right partner, and hopefully keep you excited about the journey.

THE LOGIC OF LOVE

We have established that the brain has something to do with those tingly feelings you have after knowing someone for a short period of time. As you will soon see in the Who Am I? section, we have also established that television, movies, and music have definitely influenced our views and expectations of love.

It's possible we have been working from the wrong plan. Sometimes having no plan could be just as bad as having the wrong plan. It is quite possible we had the wrong topic in our search engine. No wonder this idea of true love has eluded some of us for so long.

Let's talk about what true love could be and how it applies to long-term love and marriage.

Let's just say that to find your true love means that you found someone who is so amazing that you want to meet his/her needs. This person also thinks so highly of you that he/she wants to meet all of your needs.

Here is the most important aspect of this equation.

The person who you deem as your true love wants to meet your needs, and it has nothing to do with the fact that you want to meet his/hers. That person's desire of wanting to meet your needs is completely independent of your actions or how you treat that person.

Having your needs met is a huge contributor to your happiness, and someone's desire to see you happy is completely independent of your desire for that person. If that sounds confusing, just think of the old guy in the bank. If someone is your true love only because you meet that person's needs, that would mean—the minute you stop meeting the other person's needs—then he or she will no longer feel that bond to you.

Some people believe that true love has no reason. What that means is someone doesn't have to have a reason in order to meet your needs; that person just must decide to meet your needs. Somehow that individual has made his or her love for you a fact not a truth. He or she could come to this decision over any period of time.

That brings me to the idea of marriage. Marriage is committing to meet someone else's needs for the rest of your life. If you are his or her true love, then he or she has made the same decision. You shouldn't have to worry about getting your needs met because you are so consumed with meeting this person's needs. Keep reading as I explain.

Why would you have to worry about yourself when someone else is completely overwhelmed with taking care of your needs?

Let me be clear that I am not promoting personal neglect or looking for someone else to complete you. I have heard the phrase "I will take care of me for you if you will take care of you for me." I believe the core of this statement should be adopted by everyone looking for love. In order to have a harmonious relationship, you have to have a certain level of esteem for yourself. Later on we will discuss the blueprint to discovering your mate's needs.

A big mistake most people make during the dating process or a relationship is basing their love for someone on a specific reason. For example, loving someone because of the way the person looks, smells, sounds, behaves, etc.

Think about these statements:

"I love it when she wears tight dresses." Does this mean you won't love her when she outgrows that dress?

"I love him because he is so physically fit." Does this mean, when his body isn't as sexy, you will no longer see him in the same light?

Now I'm not suggesting that these things aren't important in the initial attraction stage. What I am saying is that it can cause problems in the future if you base your love on things that are merely truths. The phrases *I love you when*, *love how*, *love because*, and *love every time* can be dangerous statements.

I've heard world-renown pastor Myles Munroe say that these are dangerous terms because they indicate an expectation. If you have a reason for love based on something happening in the future (still wearing that formfitting dress, for example) instead of something seen in the present (shared values, shared goals, shared mindsets), that means you now have an expectation. And it is safe to say that, when you have expectations, you will oftentimes experience disappointment. Disappointment usually leads to unhappiness, because there is a disparity between your love story and your actual life.

Think about the times in your life when you expected someone to do something very important for you. Maybe there was a time you expected something important to occur. How did you feel when you were let down? I'm sure you would agree it is one of the most unpleasant feelings you have ever encountered in your life.

It is like the ultimate betrayal because, more often than not, this person was very close to you. And that disappointment will almost always lead to a divorce of your feelings for that person. It would be a great idea not to put that kind of pressure on your future love. Long-term love should be based on something completely outside of an expectation.

Again think of the old man in the bank. He would have been in the bank that day, feeling very alone, if he had an expectation in his marriage that his wife would be by his side as they lived out their final days. Can you imagine being with someone for twenty, thirty, forty years, and, the moment you can't do something you used to do together, or if you start to look different, your spouse leaves you on the spot? You have to define what love means, or what your love story is, before that time comes.

Think about the word *decide*.

If you take away the prefix "de-," you are left with the suffix "-cide." There are a few other words that end with "cide," such as suicide, homicide, and pesticide. *Suicide* is causing your own death. *Pesticide* is used to kill insects or other organisms. *Homicide* is to kill another person. So when you decide to love someone, especially in marriage, you have killed all other options.

That means that, even when you don't feel like it, you will still meet the other person's needs because you don't have any other options at this point. When I finally understood this, it was life transforming. Most of us have been sold the wrong plan. We have been given the wrong directions. Love is not solely a feeling.

So when most people blurt out their first "I love you" on the second date, they may not know everything that phrase could mean. It is a decision. It is a huge decision.

If you are going to make such a permanent decision, like marriage or spending your life with your true love, shouldn't it be based on more than how you feel at the beginning?

You will read the following statement several times throughout this book. *Most people make permanent decisions based on temporary emotions.* And they do it often. If that wasn't true, every mall you know would be out of business. We have all made an impulse purchase at some point. I'm suggesting we investigate more before we make these major purchases, such as choosing who to love for life.

FINDING YOUR EQUAL

I have heard older people say, "Marry the one who loves you, not the one you love." When I first talk with many of my clients, this is undoubtedly the most common idea they share when speaking of being happy in a relationship. It is as if the only way to be happy is to find someone who adores you.

I agree this is half of the equation, but is this really true love?

Let's break down this scenario . . .

Let's just say you marry someone who is totally in love with you. This person can't stop thinking about you and expresses this as often as possible. For some of you reading this, then your partner is always trying to meet your needs, to please you, whether it's through praise or sex. For others, your partner is doing what makes you happy, always presenting you with flowers, and constantly showing affection and commitment.

Let's just say such feelings for you are a ten on a scale of one to ten. And your feelings for your partner are a seven. Now a seven is pretty high on that scale. It's not like you are far from a ten; it's just that you don't feel the same way for your spouse as your spouse feels for you. That is not a bad relationship, but I don't believe that it is true love.

That whole idea of finding someone who loves you more is advice that was borne out of pain. Think about it. Most people rely on their feelings with regard to love and to choosing a partner. This usually means you have a 50/50 shot of either being the one who loves more or the one who is loved more. It's like playing love roulette.

When you find yourself really loving someone, and you happen to be the one who loves more, it hurts when that ends. So the best advice you would give someone, after enduring this pain, is for your friend to find someone who loves him or her more, so that you can help your friend avoid the heartbreak you have endured.

Let me just say that this is a sad life only because love offers more than that. Here is a great question I learned from one of my favorite speakers, Jim Rohn. "If you could do better, should you?" Of course my answer is yes. With that said, here is the "better."

It is possible to find a person who loves you just as much as you love him or her. It's called true love. Remember we already said how true love is meeting someone else's needs, and marriage is doing it for life. Why would you spend your life with someone who doesn't see you in the same light in which you see your partner?

Here is the challenge with being with someone who loves you more. That person will never experience the euphoric feeling of having you praise and adore them. You also suffer because you won't experience that amazing feeling of wanting to chase after and cater to them. So you actually both lose if there isn't a balance.

This is where my 60/40 principle was born. When it comes to choosing your perfect spouse, I believe you should have a balance between logic and emotion. You should focus 60 percent of your attention on logic and 40 percent on emotion when dating, when searching for your future spouse. When I say *logic*, I'm referring to this person making sense for you outside of purely just how you feel.

Since we all have a unique path to lasting love, it is difficult to put the 60/40 axiom into a step-by-step process. However, I made sure herein that it addressed three key areas: Establishing your blueprint, Controlling your thoughts and emotions and Creating your fairy tale using the 60/40 principle.

We have already spent some time explaining why emotions are important, but also why it can't be the main focus. Logic refers to the use of valid reasoning, as used in intellectual activities such as philosophy and science. Love is an intellectual activity and also a science. Throughout this book we will discuss different principles that everyone should at least know if serious about dating and finding long-term love. People are bound to repeat past failures if they do nothing to change.

I have heard the definition of *insanity* described as doing the same thing over and over again, and expecting a different result. Once you have a clear understanding of these vital principles, then you will be able to effectively use the 60/40 rule to find your ideal mate.

I remember playing with magnets as a child. It fascinated me that, if the magnets are on the correct side, they will automatically connect to one another. You don't have to push too hard; you don't have to force it. However, if you turn around one of those magnets, there is nothing you can do to get them to connect. The minute you put them close, they repel each other.

The goal of establishing your blueprint is to help you identify what you want so you can get on the correct side. Once you know what you truly want, it will be easier to attract and identify someone who is already on the correct side. You don't have to change who you are, because there is nothing wrong with you. And you don't have to change the other person, because, if you choose wisely, that person should already exhibit the qualities you seek.

Just like when you turn around the magnet, it's the same magnet. Yet I want to help you find the different side of yourself. If you are constantly repelling, maybe you need to find the other side of you.

CHAPTER SUMMARY

- What do you believe love should be, should look like in action? It is important to identify exactly what it is that you are aiming for in order to have a chance of achieving it. Keep in mind you already have a definition of what it should be (whether right or wrong), and, more than likely, the world has shaped your thoughts. Now is your time to set your course based on your own decisions of what is important to you, not those propounded by the media.

- Never blame someone or something for where you are. Take control by taking responsibility.

- Do you have unrealistic goals? Are you not working to achieve your goals and what you say you want? Is it both?

- Love is more than just how you feel. There are some scientific reasons for those feelings. You never want to make a permanent decision based on temporary emotions.

- Ideal love is based on meeting your partner's needs and your ability to get your needs met by that person. Being clear on what you want helps you to choose the person who shares your mind-set.

- Having one-sided future expectations, or those which you have never discussed with your partner, may eventually cause damage in a relationship. This is why it is also important to find someone willing to meet your needs outside of how your partner may feel. Someone who you too can meet their needs despite what you may be feeling for him or her.

- When you choose to love someone, it should be a decision. That means you have eliminated the option of leaving. With no options, it is easier for any couple to find a solution to the life challenges ahead of them.

- There is someone out there who will match your intensity when it comes to love. There is no need to play it safe by finding someone who loves you more than you love them.

WHO AM I?

THE POWER OF INFLUENCES

R ecently, I was having lunch with my father at one of my favorite restaurants. Somewhere in the conversation I started to tell him about my book, but I had no idea my thoughts would change midconversation.

I always knew that, whenever I eat a loaf of bread at home, I always skip the first one, the crusty heel, which is one of the end pieces. I would wait to eat both end pieces until they were the last two slices and I had no other choice. I started to notice that my wife would actually eat the initial end slice first. In other words, she was more than happy to eat every piece in the loaf.

So when I started to tell him where I was going with that thought, he promptly interrupted me. He said eagerly, "Well, I do that too. However, I like to save the end pieces." He proceeded to tell me how the only reason he skips the top piece and eats it with the last piece is because he thought those two fit together perfectly and made great sandwiches. And that is when it hit me.

Here is another example of how most of us have come to believe things and yet have no idea why we do. Sometimes we have no concept as to where we even got them. Here I am, for all these years, skipping the first piece of bread and not really having a reason to.

I honestly used the excuse of not liking them, but, after discussing this with my father, making a sandwich out of the two ends sounded like a great idea. I never really asked myself why I skipped to the second slice. I had no idea that my father saved the ends on purpose. Here is the even bigger shocker. I didn't even know I was copying him. WOW.

There are three ways our *love story*—the ideal we have imagined for ourselves—is shaped growing up. The first major influence is all the things we heard growing up. A few random examples include: All men are dogs. Women should do the cooking. Love is hard, etc.

The second major influence on our developing love story is what we saw growing up. With just these two forms of influence—the audible and the visible—please understand that television, music, movies, and magazines are a few of the biggest culprits. Often the people around us have been influenced by all of the above too.

The third major influence on our growing love story is what we personally experience. We have all faced some sort of despair or disappointment. The question is, how many of us still hang on to it years later?

It is a good idea to look back and challenge some of your old beliefs in order to create new ones. This type of conversation will help you to answer the following crucial questions.

- What is my love story or expectations as to true love?
- Where did I get these ideas?
- What do I want my love story to be?
- How do I get there?

Keep in mind that, in certain parts of this chapter, I'm speaking from the story I had. Later on in the book you will be able to see the stories I kept, and the new ones I created. I understand that a great actor has the ability to go back to a particular time to pull from the feelings and the emotions experienced then. I wanted to do that in this chapter. I wanted to go back and feel what I felt. This was the best way to see what my love expectation was at that time.

Another thing that I believe is important is to gain control of the memory of things that have happened to you. Oftentimes we allow our past hurts to replay in our minds over and over again, long after the actual event has taken place. Sometimes we blame circumstances and people for various reasons. If you are going to blame someone for something, at least do it on purpose. Take control of your frustration, anger, doubt, disbelief, fear, and a list of other things that could only hold you back from what you want.

Long before you can find the perfect person for you, I think it is important to discover yourself.

NEGATIVE MEMORIES THAT ARE
HOLDING YOU BACK

Before I found my future wife, I had to find me. I started by looking at my life and what contributed to my views on love and what I needed to feel complete in a relationship. I was looking to discover my love story.

Keep in mind that, if you have experienced something negative in the past with no sign of a positive meaning or gift attached thereto, it was probably because you missed the blessing in it. We live in a world of balance where there is hot and cold, day and night, as well as up and down. So it is very possible you have missed the lesson in your "misery."

In order to fully understand my perspective on love, I had to go as far back as my childhood. I had always lived with my father, two aunts, and a grandmother. My brother and I had different fathers, so he never stayed with me. He lived with our mother. I would spend weekends and sometimes entire weeks with my mother and brother who only lived twenty-five minutes away.

One day when I was twelve years old and my brother was fourteen, I called my mother's house and heard something I will never forget. My brother told me that he hadn't seen our mother in over three weeks. He also stated that he was responsible for paying the rent now.

I don't think I really grasped the magnitude of what my brother was going through at the time. As the months passed, I began to realize that our mother wasn't coming back. She had become a victim to the street life. Over the next ten years, she would be a ghost. I thought to myself, if my fourteen-year-old brother isn't showing anger toward her, why should I be angry?

It wasn't hard to recognize that my future fear regarding love and women would be that, after an extended period of time, they would lose interest in me, would leave me. I didn't understand how a mother could give birth to children and abandon them after twelve/fourteen years.

Can you see already how what I had experienced contributed to my love story?

Fast forward to my first love, my high school sweetheart. Cathy was the girl who most guys in my high school wanted to be with. She was absolutely breathtaking. A female family member of Cathy's really thought I was a great person, so this lady put in a good word for me. Before I knew it, Cathy and I were together.

Of course I felt special because, out of all the guys who wanted to be with her, she chose me. Most of my friends expressed how lucky I was that I had one of the prettiest girls around. My best friend, James, started dating Cathy's best friend, Trina. Cathy and I seemed to be perfect for each other.

Of course at the age of eighteen, I wasn't evaluating the details of whether she was my ideal partner. All I knew was that we talked all the time, and of course we had sex, which is a plus for any hormone-driven kid. I felt like an adult, and it was the most amazing feeling to be with such an amazing girl.

One day I was in the car with a few friends, including James, and we happened to see Trina. She joined us in the car, and of course James and Trina began talking. In the middle of their conversation I could tell she was very upset and bothered by something.

That's when it happened.

I heard a statement that changed my life forever. Trina said, "Trevor, you need to check on your girlfriend and her actions."

At that point all of my friends looked directly at me in disbelief. Although I tried to get more information from Trina, she insisted that I ask Cathy myself. The rest of the day seemed to move in slow motion. At this time in the world, pagers, not cell phones, were on everyone's hip. So I had to wait until I got home to call the "love of my life."

I can still see it clearly. As if it happened yesterday. I was standing by my father's bookcase when I called Cathy from a cordless phone. I was standing because I wasn't sure what I was going to hear, but in no way was I ready for what was about to happen. She was excited to hear from me as usual, so I almost felt bad for changing the direction of the call.

"I know you have something to tell me, so please just tell me, because I already know," I said.

She vehemently denied having anything to tell me, but my gut told me to be persistent. I continued to assure her that it was okay and that I just wanted to hear it from her.

Keep in mind I had no idea about what had actually happened. All I was armed with was her recently ex-best friend's vague accusation.

After pleading with Cathy for over fifteen minutes, I heard something on the other end that spoke to me louder than anything she could ever say. I heard her begin to cry. In that brief moment, I felt my young world crash. I knew I would have to sit down. I braced myself.

"Did you cheat on me?" I asked.

She proceeded to tell me that he was an older guy, and all she did was kiss him. She apologized profusely, but it didn't matter anymore. For me it was over. Despite her attempt to keep me on the phone, I had to hang up.

At that very moment all the love I had for her was gone. I never thought I would know what that feels like. My family loved this girl. This girl's family loved and respected me. How could this happen? Where did I go wrong? All I could see was my mother all over again. Of course the two had nothing to do with each other, but try telling that to the frail eighteen-year-old.

Cathy begged me to stay with her, and I wouldn't give her an answer. Because I was so crushed, I was determined to make her feel the pain I felt. We continued to speak, but it wasn't the same. By this time I was headed to college where there would be plenty of replacements, and she knew it.

We spoke for a few more weeks while I was in college, but only because she called me. I never called her. In my mind I was single. She would leave messages wondering why I wouldn't call her back. Why I wouldn't come back home to see her anymore. Why I wouldn't say *I love you*.

So a second woman had abandoned me. I had the "don't let this happen again" mentality. I was your typical "handsome young man" in college. In my mind it was time to enjoy being single. Unfortunately, by the time my next relationship came around, I didn't know how to turn off the single, scorned mentality.

This didn't allow me to be present in my next relationship. I knew that she was into me more than I was into her. I knew I loved her dearly, but I was afraid to date any woman who I loved as much as Cathy.

I had a distorted view of who I should be with. I thought it would be wise to date someone who was totally into me, unlike Cathy. The challenge is that I wasn't totally into my new girlfriend. Maybe it was because I still thought it was "cheat or be cheated on." I would do anything possible to never be in that position again. I never wanted to be so in love and caught so off guard.

My college girlfriend actually did everything right. She was the most selfless, independent person I knew. I was unable to open up to her because of my baggage. I ended up breaking her heart. I have learned to live with the pain of hurting such an amazing woman, but at the time I felt terrible. I couldn't recognize myself.

WHAT IS ABSOLUTELY NECESSARY
FOR YOU TO FEEL LOVE?

At this point in my life I was single again, and I was enjoying it. I was doing incredibly well with my business, and I felt like I was on top of the world. I said to myself that, for the next relationship I get into, I would treat that woman like a queen. To my surprise, it would be with Tracy. Someone I had already been friends with for years.

In addition to our traditional jobs, we both worked together as entrepreneurs for the same marketing company. We were around each other so much that people made assumptions that we were having sex. It is amazing because I could see why people would think that, but it just wasn't happening. I didn't see her in that light, and neither did she. She became one of my best friends, and I would even share with her stories about other women.

Here is where emotion can cause confusion. One day we were at a restaurant having dinner. As usual we were laughing uncontrollably until it happened. She had some sort of dessert that, I must admit, looked amazingly appetizing. After voicing my opinion on how great her plate looked, she did something that would change the way I felt about her.

She filled her fork with a decent portion of the pie and aimed it directly at me. Now, in my experience, most friends don't feed each other. She told me years later that she did not have romantic intentions when she did that, but, for me, it seemed as if it was an invitation. At that very moment dopamine and norepinephrine were being produced in abundance.

I honestly couldn't look at her the same anymore. I couldn't control my attraction to her. I remember hearing people say that the perfect foundation for a love relationship should be a friend relationship. What better woman to have on my arm than my best friend at the time?

So of course I made the necessary moves to make her my girlfriend. To be romantically with a woman I was once friends with seemed like all anyone would need to create a successful relationship.

About two months into the relationship, I was sitting in the computer lab with Tracy. At this time Facebook required you to have a school address in order to register. We were both new to Facebook, and I had just learned how to change my dating status to "in a relationship."

I can still remember what happened next like it was yesterday. I just happened to notice on her screen that her relationship status still displayed Single. I wasn't upset or bothered in any way. I just thought maybe she didn't notice or maybe she didn't know how to change it. So to satisfy my curiosity, I did what any good man would do. I asked her.

"Why haven't you changed your relationship status?"

Now let me say, I didn't think anything was wrong with her response then, and I still don't. She said to me, "I don't like people in my business." I know plenty of people now that are in long-term committed relationships and still haven't changed their Facebook status. So this was in no way an indication of someone cheating or not being totally into you. However, let me express to you the thought that ran circles around my brain.

Throughout my life I have seen how a woman reacts to being in a relationship with a guy she is totally into. Even if they are not in a relationship, most woman are more than excited to express to the world that they are associated with a guy that they are dating. I know that is a huge generalization, but, remember, for me, I needed as much certainty as possible in order to feel comfortable giving my all.

Just understand, by this point in my life, I had dated enough women to recognize when one was totally into me. I had also been in the position where I had a crush on a woman who didn't care that much about returning the attention I was giving. I was superromantic. I was superconfident.

I had already made up my mind that the next girlfriend I had would get my full attention. So I was certain I did everything in those first two months that most girls would die for. With that said, Tracy's response completely shocked me. What kind of woman wouldn't want people to know that she was dating me? I remember saying to myself, she is not the one for me, because I don't do it for her.

I felt that at the core of my spirit. I had felt it prior to the computer lab, but now it was clear to me. I almost knew for a fact that I should run at that point. For some reason I didn't. Maybe it was because we were best friends. Maybe it was because I had already made up my mind that I would make my next relationship work. Maybe I wanted to avoid reliving that rejection from my mother and from Cathy.

Hear this. Most people would rather feel like they did something wrong than to feel like the person they love desires someone else. If it's something I'm not doing, then there is a sense of hope that I can fix it. If someone desires someone else, there is little chance that you can fix that to benefit you. And human beings are creatures of hope.

I also remember thinking I could have been making a big deal out of nothing. Basically I second-guessed my first instinct. What I would later call my personal logic or my "gut." I knew that I wanted a woman who was totally into me, and here is the first clue to send me packing, and what did I do? I decided to work for her love and ultimately the attention I wanted from her instead of finding a woman who already had what I was looking for.

It reminds me of a story I heard years ago. If someone gave you a deck of cards and told you to find four aces as quick as possible, what would you do? Some people would just simply flip through the entire deck and pull out the four aces as they came upon them.

Obviously this is the best possible method to accomplish this task.

There are some people who are so smart that they would pull out a Magic Marker to change into aces the first four cards they find. The challenge with that is, no matter how great their artistic ability, those cards are still not aces. I guess you could say that I was the second person in that example.

Again this doesn't mean that there was anything wrong with Tracy. What it did mean was that she wasn't exactly what I was looking for, but that didn't stop me from pulling out the Magic Marker.

For the next three years I spent a large portion of our relationship enjoying the fact that I could come home to my best friend. I also spent a great deal of time filled with doubt. I had taken on this challenge to make her fall for me the way I thought a woman should.

I had created the biggest expectation that she could never live up to because it just wasn't her role to play as my future wife, my true love. I showered her with attention, romance, and genuine love. However, her lack of passion for me was obvious, and it was the most painful feeling ever.

To me it just appeared that she would eventually find the guy who stirred that passion inside her, because I felt I couldn't. Call it irony but you can attract into your life exactly what you focus on.

One day we were sitting in the car, and I said to her, "I think we should break up, because I don't feel like you really love me." What I now understand is that I should have said, "You don't love me the way I want you to."

I could have said, "With you I do not feel the way I absolutely need to feel when it comes to love." There is a huge difference. She clearly loved me; she just wasn't the right woman for me.

She then did something I rarely saw her do. She began to cry. I was blown away. I didn't know what to think. But I can tell you what I felt. "Wow, she really does love me." I mean, why would she cry over losing me, right? I now wanted it to work so bad that I was looking for any good sign. I just knew that her attention toward me would be different moving forward.

The challenge was that this new Tracy remained in my imagination. I had two options: either leave or cheat. Of course an unoccupied mind is a vulnerable one. That's when I made the mistake of telling another woman about the challenges I was having. A few weeks passed by and this young lady continuously gave me the attention that Tracy wasn't.

Then one day this woman said the most shocking statement I ever heard from another female at the time. "For everything your woman is not willing to do, there is another woman willing to do it, and I'm that woman." Wow. It was as if she knew exactly what I wanted to hear. At this point I was an attention-deprived twentysomething-year-old man. I remember thinking, why doesn't Tracy feel the same way?

Around this time I cheated on her. After I forced myself to see the wrongdoing in my infidelity, I beat myself up so much to the point where I had convinced myself that I deserved to be in the situation I was in. Sure I wasn't getting what I wanted, but that was no reason to cheat on my best friend. I began to shower Tracy with love even more. I was already doing better than any other man she had ever been with at the time. Now my guilt propelled me to be better.

Around the four-year mark of our relationship, nothing had really changed at all. It was a strange balance. I still wasn't getting the passionate woman I thought I deserved. Most people want to feel needed. Although I was unhappy in certain areas of my life, I can easily say that we had a blast around each other.

Another challenge started to arise. By now I was so unhappy, I began to entertain text messages from other women. The challenge was, I wasn't feeling it from the woman I was with. I have always been a believer in "If you change the way you look at things, the things you look at will change."

So I thought it would be best to stick with Tracy and just work on me. Over the course of our entire relationship, I had read at least seventy-plus books on success, relationships, and love. However, the information wasn't enough for me to ignore my need to be desired.

Being respected and admired is a big deal for most people and especially for me. There were several women who consistently praised me and expressed an interest in me. Since I wasn't receiving that kind of attention at home, I embraced it from other sources. I'm sure if I had continued any longer, it would have turned into more.

Here is where the story takes a turn.

INTUITION SOMETIMES SCREAMS AT YOU

I had upgraded my phone, so I no longer needed my older one. One day I came home and realized Tracy was not home, but there was a note on the stairs. The note was a list of a few women Tracy had discovered I had been in contact with.

I was not sleeping with these women, but I was clearly flirting and being inappropriate. The crazy part about it was, she got this list from the older phone I was no longer using. Something in her gut caused her to go searching.

What makes it even stranger was that the phone no longer possessed a battery. I later found out that Tracy had found my old phone and had plugged it into a charger, and it had worked without the battery. I honestly didn't even know that was possible. I could tell she had left the house in anger.

The first thing I did was call my mentor and longtime friend, Omar. He was also an entrepreneur within the same marketing company as Tracy and I. He also knew Tracy, so I figured he would be able to help me reach her.

Omar had taught me many lessons in my financial career, and his mother called me *son* since I was so close to his family. Omar's younger brother had died years earlier, and since then he would call me his younger brother. I felt honored because I knew how close he was to his siblings.

He always seemed to have the right answers, so, when I saw Tracy's note on the steps, there was no doubt in my mind who I should call first. Omar assured me that he would speak to her on my behalf. When he finally got in touch with her, he told me exactly what I needed to do.

When Tracy finally came home, I could see the anger in her eyes. The names she confronted me with were not the issue. The two women I had actually cheated on her with were not on her list. The text messages she found in my old phone were just that: text messages.

I took it upon myself to tell her what had happened years ago. I told her who I had an affair with and when. Of course this was years prior, but naturally the pain for her was just as bad as if it happened that day. She was crushed.

I think she may have cried for two days straight. To her knowledge, she had never been cheated on before, so this was the first time she had ever experienced such pain. I knew that was part of the reason she could never really appreciate everything I did for her, but I didn't expect to be the one to break her heart.

Anyone who knew me personally knew that all I wanted to do was make our love work. However, through years of frustration, I began to go against my original goal of treating my next woman like a queen. How would I get our relationship back to that original point? I can't say cheating was a habit because I had been faithful for over two and a half years.

By now three days of silence had passed, and Tracy finally shared what was on her mind. She told me that she forgave me. She also expressed that she understood my dissatisfaction with certain things in our relationship. I had spoken to her friends and her family over the years, just trying to get a better understanding of who she was and what I could do to be the guy who she desired.

With that said, she was still shocked that I had actually cheated on her, and, since my credibility was now in question, she didn't believe that it had only happened with two people.

Over the next three months things got slightly better. I credited part of this to the help of my good friend Omar who had been speaking to her and edifying how much I loved her on my behalf. At this point we were about three months away from our destination wedding.

One day we were at an event out of town for our marketing company. Tracy was standing in line to grab us a few drinks, and Omar was standing in front of her. I thought, why are they so close to each other? But I quickly ignored the thought because I felt foolish. After all, Omar was helping me regain her trust. I had asked this guy to be in my wedding. I just knew now that my insecurity was getting the best of me.

Later that night when we were back in our room, I stayed up a little later than I wanted to. To my surprise her phone vibrated with a phone call. When I reached over to grab the phone for her, the name of the caller was on the display; it was Omar. Of course I was confused as to why my good friend Omar would be calling her at 3:00 a.m. in the morning, but I decided to let it go.

When we returned home from the conference, I decided to call Omar and asked him why he was calling her. He then told me that she had expressed some concern about staying with me and that he was following up with her at that time since he knew we were both up. I was still unsure of his answer, so I asked him, "Are you sleeping with Tracy?"

He responded with a breath of disbelief. "I would never do something like that, *dawg*. You are my brother." He expressed how shocked he was that I would accuse him of something so serious. Honestly I was shocked that I would accuse him of something like that as well. We had known each other for years. I began to feel that maybe I had developed insecurities because of my own cheating. I even thought maybe it was the fear of being abandoned again like my mother had done. Like Cathy had done.

After a few weeks Tracy and I started having conversations about breaking up again. This time she was the one to initiate them. This was shocking because we had already booked our trip for the wedding, and several family members had booked their trips as well. We were now starting to feel the pressure of making such a permanent decision. I thought maybe she couldn't really get over the fact that I had cheated on her.

We sat in our bedroom, and she told me that she has never really felt like she was in love with me and that she wanted to feel that passion for her man. She had never experienced those "butterflies" for me. Of course, I had noticed that two months into the relationship but had ignored it.

Still I have to admit that I felt crushed. I just couldn't imagine how all my efforts to make this woman happy had failed. We would continue to have conversations over the next few days surrounding this subject, what she called a "lack of intimacy."

I couldn't understand why we lacked it, because, at the time, no one knew her better than me, and no one knew me better than her. What she was really saying was she lacked that euphoric feeling for me. It felt nothing like a fairy tale.

April 21, 2009, was a day I will never forget.

It was my birthday, but, more important than that, it was a day that would change my view of love forever. While I was at my traditional job, Tracy and I continued our conversations about the fate of our relationship. Most of this occurred over text messages, but we had finally agreed to just call it quits.

I was making plans to go to our apartment complex to take my name off the lease as soon as I got home the next day. I was so disappointed in what now seemed like wasted time. I knew we would have to call our parents to cancel their trips for our wedding, which wasn't happening now. I knew I would have to find a new apartment.

And I also knew that, even though I had planned on making my next relationship work, this one was ending in a ball of flames on my birthday. Not only was my heart hurt but my pride was hurt, since my woman of four years could honestly say she was never in love with me. I had no idea what that meant at the time, but it sounded horrible.

Since it was my birthday, everyone was excited to go out to lunch to celebrate, except me. I didn't want anyone to know what I was going through, because I was so used to people looking to me for guidance on life's challenges.

I was ashamed to let anyone know I had a major challenge of my own. Everyone at work also expected me to be married in two months. I had no idea how to explain why I would no longer be getting married.

It seemed like a unanimous decision to head to Longhorn Steakhouse for my birthday lunch. I was filled with negative emotions, and now I would have to try to hide them from twelve people as we sat and ate lunch.

I think I did a pretty good job concealing my true pain from everyone except Rashawna, who was one of my coworkers. I laughed along with everyone and contributed to the conversation as if nothing were wrong. Rashawna looked me in the eye. Without her saying a word, I could read her lips. *What's wrong?*

How did she know something was wrong? How could she see past my smile to recognize the pain that I had tried so badly to bury?

All I could do was shake my head and try to lie to her, but it was apparent that she wasn't buying it for a second. I was amazed that she could see what eleven other people couldn't. As soon as we got back to work, Rashawna tried her best to console me.

I assured her everything was okay and that I would tell her in time. It was impossible to control the thoughts that were running through my head, and I was trying my best to come up with a plan to get through this, but nothing could prepare me for what was about to happen next.

I remember my mentor and close friend Omar using this phrase often: coincidence is God's way of staying anonymous. Basically God won't come down from the sky and give you exactly what you want. In most cases God will use things in your life to give you guidance toward your purpose.

I clearly remember a voice in my head that distracted me from typing on my keyboard. The voice was quiet but firm, and it said to me, check her email. In the past, when I have heard stories of people hearing the voice of or receiving messages from God, it had always sounded like a lie. However, this voice seemed like it came directly from God. It may have just been my subconscious mind pushing me in the direction of looking for evidence.

At this point it was early afternoon, and I couldn't help but feel like my world was falling apart. I had dedicated all of my energy to this woman, and she was now leaving the relationship. Not only did she seem excited about her new life without me, but she showed no emotions that indicated she would miss me. Talk about crushing my pride.

Finally I gave in. I decided to check her email. I had always had her password but had never really felt the need to use it. Years ago she gave it to me to check something for her, and I thought her password was so clever and funny that I naturally committed it to memory.

Typing in her password must have taken an hour because it seemed like an eternity. It was probably because I was nervous. I was afraid of what I would see on the opposite side of this log-in screen. However you choose to look at it, what happened next was nothing short of a miracle.

Once I opened the in-box, I didn't notice anything out of the ordinary. I immediately remember feeling like a loser for even going this far. I had always laughed at men when they said their woman checked their guy's cell phone or email, and here I was stooping to that same level.

I decided to click on the Sent items. I can tell you that I will never forget this. It was the true beginning of my purpose, but I had no idea at the time. There it was at the top of the list. I saw an email that had a subject title that read *Hey, baby*. It wasn't my email address that was listed as the recipient.

In fact, it was an email address that looked very familiar. Yep, you guessed it. It was Omar. My heart fell to the floor. I can't lie. I stared at the subject title for about five minutes. I had no thoughts. I just remember not being able to breathe. I've never had an anxiety attack, but I can only imagine that had to be what I experienced.

After a few minutes I realized I couldn't fix my breathing challenge, so I just started reading the email. Although I don't remember everything that was said verbatim, I do know the basic message. She expressed how much fun she had had the other night, but she felt horrible for what she had been doing for the past few weeks.

She had longed to feel that euphoric feeling with a man, and she was excited that she was now feeling it with Omar. Tracy expressed that I had done my share of wrongdoings, but I was a great man and didn't deserve to be treated this way.

Anyone reading this can imagine how crushed my pride was at this time. There is nothing more demoralizing to a person's spirit like hearing that your partner not only isn't into you but is into one of your close friends who was also your mentor. He was older than me. He made more money than me. In my mind I was just not good enough.

With that anger I printed out the email, and, without alerting my boss or any of my coworkers, I ran to my car and headed to her job. I called her as soon as I got in the car. "Do you have something to tell me?" Of course she acted as if there were nothing out of the ordinary, but I was persistent. When I mentioned Omar's name, she immediately said, "I knew you were going to check my email."

Here is the most amazing thing about this story. She told me that, directly after she had sent the email, she had deleted it. I'm assuming she didn't want to have evidence sitting around.

I'm not sure if you understand what I'm saying, but that would mean that I checked her email within the ten seconds it took for her to click Send, go to her Sent messages, and delete it. Wow. No one can tell me that there wasn't a higher power working at that moment, trying to get a message to both of us. I can't even begin to calculate the odds. What were the chances that I would see that message?

Over the next few days, I filled my time with negative thoughts. I couldn't even confront Omar because he was out of the country on vacation. I believe God wanted me to gather myself so that I wouldn't make a permanent decision based on temporary emotion. Who knows what I would have done if I had encountered him in those first few days?

The next few months were nothing short of impossible. I still don't have a clear reason as to why I did what I did, but I can tell you now that I am so grateful.

A good friend of mine, named Thomas, would be one of the people I turned to in this darkest hour. He was someone I respected just as much as I respected Omar. At this point I felt like I couldn't trust anyone. Thomas had admitted to going through infidelity in his marriage in the past and was now one of the happiest married men I know.

A part of me wanted to believe that this was the thing my relationship with Tracy needed to transcend the mediocrity we had been living. If Thomas and his wife could turn such a negative event into a positive one, then I felt Tracy and I could do the same.

People would ask me, "So when are you moving out?" Once they found out that I was still staying in the house, they were shocked. Some people of course labeled me crazy. Some people admired my resilience but expected me to eventually change my mind.

No one could understand how I could face such deceit and stay with Tracy. Furthermore, everyone couldn't understand how this could happen. Omar was not only a close friend but we were always together.

On the outside, it appeared as if my life had never changed. I would show up to business meetings and trainings with more energy than anyone in the room. I cannot tell you how many times someone asked me how I was able to move on so quickly and continue to succeed.

In my head I could only think of one of my favorite quotes. *In order to lead an orchestra, you must first turn your back to the crowd.* I knew that it wouldn't be easy, but, in order to be great, I would have to overcome major setbacks. I began to look at this as the path I was given, and my job was to learn from it and to become great because of it.

I was always big on training others on the topic of personal development within our insurance company. I felt some sort of responsibility to those people I had been training. How could I talk to them about never quitting and then give up myself? How could I teach people how to face adversity and be the one to run at the first sign of it?

It wasn't long at all before people started calling me and sharing their own personal issues. People opened up to me about things no one would ever know. I believe people began to look to me for leadership, because it is very rare to have someone who does exactly what they teach.

The only challenge was, I was not as complete as I appeared. Sure, when I spoke at meetings, trainings, or weekly conference calls, I would amaze people with lessons that would help them create the life they truly wanted and deserved. However, on the inside I was slowly dying. In my mind, I felt like the biggest failure. I had never felt this feeling before. And the crazy thing was, no one could honestly tell except Thomas and Tracy.

Thomas knew I was a walking emotional wreck because we spoke almost every day for what seemed like two months. I think he felt a responsibility to guide me as much as he could. He would share different things with me about how he and his wife were able to rise above their infidelity challenges, and I became inspired.

I no longer looked at Tracy the same way, but she was now going above and beyond to make up for her recent actions.

For a brief moment in time, I started to feel the love and attention that I knew I wanted in my woman. That same feeling that hadn't been there as early as two months into our relationship. Thomas often forewarned me that it would not last, because she would go back to who she was, once she had earned back my love. Even though he and his wife had made it through their own crisis, Thomas wanted me be aware that there were no guarantees. And to guard my own sense of happiness.

So, if I wanted to be happy, it couldn't be based solely on how she was treating me during this process.

He was right, because what would happen if she stopped her efforts to win me over? Does that mean I go back to being unhappy? I did not want my happiness to be defined by a truth. So I had to find another route to discovering myself—or better yet, creating myself—because I honestly was at zero.

Over the four years we were together, I read more than seventy books and journals on relationships and success in general. I was always willing and eager to apply what I thought would benefit our relationship. Since all those books and seminars were not enough to help prevent an event like this, I was open to taking a different route to success at love.

Thomas had suggested that I speak to a marriage counselor. When I heard what she charged for an hour of her time, I honestly thought to myself, maybe I should read another book. At least that was a cheaper option.

I clearly didn't understand the magnitude of having a coach. Reluctantly I hired her for one hour, and she spent most of the time feeling me out. She obviously needed to get to know me and my situation.

Although she had counseled many married couples, she was amazed at my commitment to making this work. All of her research and experience had told her that most men can't get through their wives' infidelities. I took on the challenge of being one of the few like Thomas.

Through counseling, I started to discover a little about myself. I learned that, because my mother had walked out of my life when I was eleven, I was quite possibly trying my best to avoid that feeling of being abandoned again.

After all, Tracy had just done the unthinkable, yet I felt that she would never do it again. If I moved on to another woman, she could easily cheat on me. It was almost safer for me to stay where I was.

Obviously this was not a smart reason to stay with someone, but again this was the story I told myself. I honestly had never allowed myself to miss my mother, because I probably couldn't deal with the fact that she could walk out of my life and never look back.

Most of my friends had experienced their fathers leaving the family. Mothers were supposed to be connected to their children, right? So how could my mother leave my brother and I? How could she choose a life of drugs and the streets over her two boys?

One thing was for sure. I started to believe there was something wrong with me if a woman could care so little about how I felt as a son or a fiancé.

One of the things I loved most about my relationship coach was that she never tried to tell me what I should or shouldn't do. The thing I love about coaching is that a good coach usually asks the right questions to cause you to create your own answers and advice. Sure, it may seem like you could just pay yourself to do it, but it never really happens. This is why there are coaches in professional sports. You need someone who can see the whole field/court while you are playing so hard on it.

One of the best questions, in two forms, that she asked me was "What does your gut tell you? What does your logic say?"

I had never really thought about that, since I thought relationships were simply matters of the heart. I couldn't imagine how far we would get just by talking about logic.

Another lesson learned was, it is very difficult to separate logic and emotions when you are emotionally involved with someone. I truly thought my logic wanted me to work things out. My brain was telling me that most married couples fight through their challenges, and this was just one of those things you have to go through and to grow through.

What I've realized was that my emotions were trying to avoid pain and the dangerous unknown. After all, because Tracy was now working hard to win me over, I felt like I was on cruise control, and I wouldn't have to work as hard anymore. Why would I go somewhere else and have to start all over again?

The only challenge was, I was still very unhappy with her. It seemed like every other day I would bring up the situation again. I bombarded Tracy with questions because

I wanted to know more. I really wanted to inform my logic and somehow find closure, but it wasn't working as quickly as I had wanted it to.

I attended several parties with her, and, in the midst of everyone having a great time, I would just ruin the night by becoming totally upset with her. I would constantly question her love for me and her commitment, even though she was doing everything possible to show me that she had made the same mistake I had made, and she was just as sorry as I was.

THERE WAS A BLESSING WITHIN YOUR CHAOS

Please understand that we all have a story to tell. Some of you may have grown up in a single-parent household or experienced domestic abuse—seeing your parents inflict physical harm on each other or were a victim directly. Some of you may share a similar story to me. I revealed a part of my story to serve as your guide when reviewing what has shaped your love story and how to write your own blueprint.

As a result of my experiences, I was later able to determine everything I would need to be happy in a relationship. Take a quick glance back at your life and evaluate the things that have shaped who you are and how you love. Although I did not share every detail of my story, let me give you a few examples of what I have learned by reviewing my life, so you can hopefully gain clarity for yourself.

Notice that these things I needed go beyond the typical superficial list most people come up with when describing what they want in a partner or what they need from love. You often hear women describe a man who is six two and makes six figures, while some men require a woman to be shaped like a runway model or have long luxurious hair. More than likely these things have been beaten into their head by the many media influences paraded in front of us since birth.

In most cases these things aren't really important. Looking back at your experiences allows you to see exactly what has happened and how it has affected you. This allows you to create a life that is tailor-made for you.

Remember, as I discussed in the True Love section, it is important to define what you are looking for before you begin dating, so you can truly evaluate if this person will be a potential match. When considering what I wanted, here are just a few areas that I began focusing on:

1. I knew I wanted a woman who wanted children and her reason had nothing to do with me. I have heard many young women express their fear of what pregnancy would do to their body. I can totally understand that, which is why I wouldn't want that pressure on me. I wouldn't want my wife to resent me because of what a baby did to her body. I wanted

a woman who felt part of her purpose was to have children.

2. I also realized that having a woman totally into me was important. I knew I wanted a woman who was emotionally moved by me, and it wasn't a result of something I was directly doing. Sure, I can be a very romantic guy, but I didn't want her emotional attachment to me to be tied to what I was doing. I didn't feel I should have to apologize for knowing what I needed to be happy in a long-term relationship. I couldn't imagine having to endure again the disappointment of knowing the woman I loved didn't feel like she was in love with me.

3. I knew I wanted a woman who felt like part of her purpose was to be a wife, like I looked forward to being a good husband. I believed that a wife would take great pride in living to meet her husband's needs, as I would meet hers, and I'm not just speaking sexually. She would take great pride in representing me every time she walked out of the house. She would desire working hand-in-hand with me when it comes to healthy eating, caring for others, earning and saving money, along with a list of other things. I was preparing for marriage and was seeking a woman who was equally preparing for marriage, with shared goals and mind-sets.

I remember having a conversation with my father that would alter the way I viewed life. I told him how hard it was to fight through the challenges I was having, and I was shocked that he didn't side with me. He simply told me to stop torturing her. He forced me to realize that it was my decision to stay with her. Therefore, it was not fair to continually bring up the past. He then told me one of the most profound statements I have ever heard.

"If you don't like something, then change it. If you can't change it, there is absolutely no reason to stress over it."

With these words I began to realize that I couldn't go back in the past and change what had already happened. It was now time to find a way to relieve the stress I was causing myself.

CHAPTER SUMMARY

- The way we approach life has usually been given to us. It is up to you to identify what you believe and change it if those initial beliefs don't get you where you want to be.
- Identifying the blessing in every situation drastically changes the course of your life. That relationship/event happened to teach you something.
- Discover/Decide who you want to be in your life. Strategically line up your life/habits to match that person you wish to become.
- Sometimes your gut will tell you something, but oftentimes it is your insecurity talking. Try to distinguish between the two.
- Get help to develop into who you were destined to become.
- Use your past as a guiding tool to discover what you truly want.

STOP MAKING UP S*%!

CONTROLLING YOUR EMOTIONS

I have learned to trust my gut when it comes to some of life's events. Yet I believe it would be very difficult to go with my gut if I continued to allow my thoughts to be on autopilot.

There are people who get strong feelings of jealousy, and they often attribute those feelings as a warning from their gut. My simple yet complex question would be: how do you know it is a genuine gut feeling?

The next two chapters are dedicated to helping you understand how to get to the point where you can trust yourself and your thoughts.

Sometimes it is easy to believe that our emotions and our thoughts are on autopilot. At least that is what I thought. Shortly after surviving the most emotionally catastrophic event in my life, I believe God sent me my first life raft.

My job at the time wanted me to expand my leadership skills. They funded my trip out of town to attend a two-day course that was designed for leaders who are in charge of large projects for a few major companies. In this class I saw CEOs, directors, and project managers who were all learning the same lessons. I had no idea that some of the skills I would learn would not only apply to the challenges I was having in my love life but it would take my job and my business to the next level.

There were two topics that really stood out to me. The first topic was called Controlling Your Thoughts, Emotions & Results. I'm sad that I can't even remember the angel who was teaching the class. I wish I could thank her again and tell her just how much her insights changed my life forever.

Sometimes negative emotions can fall on us like being caught in a rainstorm. It's hard to focus on anything if you are standing in the rain with no umbrella. For me, the rain was pouring in my life at this time, and, for a few months, I had no refuge or shelter. She was the one who handed me the umbrella (information) that I would soon use to protect me from the downpour and to allow me to actually see clearly.

Before this class, I spent more time wiping the rain from my face (thinking of all the things wrong with my life) than actually seeing what was in front of me (appreciating all the blessings in my life). Of course I wasn't out of the storm yet, but at least I was now armed with some cover.

When controlling your emotions, there are a series of steps and processes that your brain goes through. Keep in mind, this process occurs in your life every day, every hour, and sometimes every minute. Even as you read this book, this process is happening.

The five steps in order are as follows:

1. An Event Happens.
2. You Respond with Self-Talk.
3. Emotions Follows.
4. Leading to Behavior.
5. Resulting in an Outcome.

Step one, an event occurs.

An event could be an email notification coming through on your phone. It could be something as simple as you tripping as you run up a flight of stairs on your way to the cafeteria. It could be a car just cut you off on the highway, or it could be something as traumatic as finding out your spouse of fifteen years has been cheating on you.

On any given day there could be dozens of events that occur in your life. Now keep in mind that, when an event happens, it doesn't have a meaning. I know most people will be confused by that statement but really think about it. We give it a meaning based on our life experiences, knowledge, television, music, friends, etc.

The meaning we give this event doesn't make it correct just because other people agree with you. It only means that you and others have given the same meaning to a particular event.

Most people have encountered a baby screaming at some point in their life. It is interesting to see how many different meanings people will give to such an event.

The father says, "The baby is hungry."
The mother says, "The baby is sleepy."
The grandmother says, "The baby is teething."
The grandfather says, "The baby is hot."

Now all of the above could possibly be true at any given time, but what if they were all wrong this time? What if the baby heard Elmo sing a song on television and wanted to duplicate the soft, soothing sound?

Since most babies have not learned how to formulate a full sentence yet, instead of a happy song being projected, to most of the adults in the room, it sounded like a baby crying. I know this example may seem far-fetched, but my point is that you give an event meaning based on who you are and what you believe at the time of observation.

Here is another example of someone giving meaning to a meaningless event. Let's say you and a group of friends are hanging out late at a local lounge. Out of nowhere your friend Bill stumbles down the last three stairs in the hallway.

One of your friends says, "Bill must have had too much to drink."

Another friend says, "He tripped over his shoelaces."

What if Bill just missed a step because the hallway had such dim illumination along the staircase?

By now you get the point that, when something happens, it doesn't mean anything until you give it a meaning.

When a car swerves off the road, it doesn't mean anything until you give it a meaning.

When your spouse cheats on you, it doesn't mean anything until you give it a meaning.

When a store clerk doesn't respond to your enthusiastic "Good morning," it doesn't mean anything until you give it a meaning.

The next step is where interpretation, or meaning, is given to a meaningless event.

This leads directly into the second step of self-talk. This step is the most important of the five steps because it controls everything. This is where the controlling-emotions process truly starts, because this is where you have complete control over how the situation will play out.

When you hear the term "self-talk," what is the first thing that comes to mind?

Talking to yourself?

Of course we all talk to ourselves at some point during the day, but, in this case, we are talking about a deeper level of dialogue. You have already learned that, when an event happens, it does not have a meaning until we give it a meaning. This can be referred to as your perception of the event.

The amazing thing about a person's perception is that, even if it is totally wrong, it is still considered reality by that person. I'm sure there was a time when you didn't feel very confident in your appearance, but, because we are our biggest critics, no one else noticed any "flaws" but you.

Our perception becomes our reality. If we feel there is something wrong with the way we look, there is nothing that anyone can do to change that, because we can never live beyond the limits of our beliefs. Instead of the words "perception" or "interpretation," I prefer to use the term "self-talk" because it is a more accurate depiction of what actually goes on in our head.

To explain self-talk, let's use an example that recently occurred with two close friends of mine named Patrice and her boyfriend, James. They were in a long-distance relationship with Patrice living in New York and James living in Virginia. Since I was friends with both of them, Patrice and James sought my advice on dating.

One day Patrice called me in a state of panic. I could hear the frustration in her voice as she began to tell me what was bothering her.

"Trevor, that's it. I can't take it anymore. I know he is cheating on me." She proceeded to tell me that, thirty minutes prior to calling me, she had reached out to James on his cell phone. Since he didn't answer the phone immediately, she decided to call him right back. Two minutes later he sent her a text which read: I will give you a call in a little while.

The reason she needed to speak with him so badly was because she was having a major family issue, and all she wanted to do was talk to her "better half" so she could feel comforted. Since she was at least five driving hours from him, it was very important to her that he answer the phone whenever she called.

Of course this was probably part of her love story, and her actual life wasn't matching it at this time. This particular element of her love story allowed her to feel secure that he wasn't with other women. She obviously has some insecurity because her last boyfriend had cheated on her every chance he could get. It didn't help that this same ex-boyfriend lived five minutes away from her.

I could imagine in her mind how she probably thought James had a different woman every night. Since I was also friends with James, I actually knew that he was totally happy being faithful and committed to her. I also knew that he refused to jeopardize his relationship by being unfaithful.

Let's examine the situation.

The event was James didn't answer his phone and sent Patrice a text. Let's stop right there. From Patrice's standpoint, technically that has no meaning. Well, it shouldn't have had any meaning. Patrice's self-talk probably told her that James must be cheating, because, if he wasn't, he would call back and not text. Wow. When I later called James, I discovered that he couldn't answer the phone because he was heavily engaged with a project he was working on. Where did Patrice get her idea from then?

Look at what Patrice told herself about James not picking up the phone. Look what she made that mean in her head. You can imagine if a person's mind automatically has a negative self-talk, it could make for a very negative day. Having enough negative days can ultimately lead to living a negative life.

Self-talk, whether it's negative or positive, will always create some sort of emotion. Emotion is the third step in this process. Let's imagine your emotions are the most beautiful flowers the earth could provide. In order for these seeds to grow into flowers and blossom, there are a few things that are required.

One of the first things you will need is soil. You will also need plenty of sunlight, water, and maybe even fertilizer. Well, if your emotions are the flowers, self-talk is undoubtedly the seed. You will get in your life what you plant. If you give an event a negative meaning, you will have a negative emotion. If you give an event a positive meaning, which equates to positive self-talk, you will have a positive emotion.

Have you ever had a negative emotion toward someone?

I'm sure someone has pissed you off in the past. Can you remember how excited that made you? I don't mean excited in a good way. I'm referring to the time you were so angry emotionally that you could feel it physically. It is a feeling that could derail your entire day. That is a horrible place to be simply because feeling stressed, depressed, or angry is a recipe for an unhappy life.

Let's go back to my two friends Patrice and James. It is obvious that Patrice's negative emotions have consumed her. She has no idea that she is the cause of this pain. Her perception has now become reality, even though it isn't reality.

This isn't an easy concept for most people to get, but it is probably one of the most important things you could master.

Think of the time you were cheated on. Think about the time you lost someone close to you. These events don't bring along positive emotions. And until now you had no control over your emotions. What if maybe, just maybe, you had a different self-talk about those events?

I'm not saying it is easy to do, but think about how your life would be transformed if you could control the conversation going on in your mind. Perhaps the major events that will later occur in your life could be given a positive meaning. I use the term "major" loosely because whether something is classified as major or minor is determined by the meaning you give it.

All of the steps that we have gone over take place in your mind. So far, the world has no idea how you are interpreting, thinking, or feeling.

Behavior is the fourth step of this process. Behavior can be defined as a variety of mannerisms and actions made by a person. You have seen many different people in your life behave or act in a certain way. Now you should have some insight on what caused those behaviors. It was their emotions.

I heard this statement years ago at a leadership seminar. You should write it down and put it somewhere in your house so you can see it often until it's stuck in your head.

"Some people make permanent decisions based on temporary emotions."

Just think, if people never based their decisions on temporary emotions, malls would go out of business. Think of how many people had a passionate night together when that temporary emotion was high. As a result of that temporary emotion, there could have been a child brought into the world. I would say having a child is a permanent decision.

I'm sure there would be less crime and violence if some people just realized that you may not always feel the way you are feeling right now. There are plenty of people in prison because they acted on a feeling which they no longer have. In the world our actions speak so loud that no one can hear what we are saying. However, it is extremely difficult to control your actions when the emotion is so strong. When you are upset, it is a challenge for you to rid yourself of the desire to voice or act out your opinion.

You can already see how upset Patrice was, but remember, up until this point, only she knows that. Here is the amazing thing about this entire process. If you regain control of the steering wheel of your life before it gets to the "behavior" section, you can avoid a catastrophic collision. After she expressed to me that she felt James was cheating, it was obvious what she was thinking. It was clear to me at this point that those thoughts had already produced an emotion that wasn't a pleasant one.

Remember James couldn't answer her call so he sent her a quick text letting her know he would call her back shortly. Her immediate action reflected her self-talk. Her reply text read: I will call you tomorrow, since you are just too busy for me. Of course her response was uncalled-for, but people make permanent decisions based on temporary emotions all the time.

After he received that text, James dropped everything he was doing and called her to see what was wrong. Since she was so upset at this point, she ignored his call. James informed me that he figured she didn't want to talk, and he would just wait for her call in the morning. Of course Patrice was even angrier because, by now, another event (or nonevent) had taken place.

Apparently she had expected him to call back a second time, and, when he didn't, she had self-talk about that lack of an expected event as well. All he did was refrain from calling her a second time and honored her wish of speaking tomorrow. Her emotions transformed her into being sarcastic and rude to a devoted boyfriend.

Patrice did what most people do with meaningless events and gave it a meaning. Even though she has since apologized for blowing things out of proportion, she can never take back her actions. Now her thoughts and emotions have been expressed to the world in physical form.

Your thoughts are no longer just in your head when you act out how you thought and felt about an event. You never get a second chance to make a first impression. Of course they were months past a first impression; however, relationships are made of thousands of first impressions grouped together.

You have to control the fairy tale called "your relationship." This is the perfect romantic movie, and you are the lead role and the director. You have to wake up every morning and make another first impression.

It is about creating a space or being in a position where you never exhaust the possibilities. You bring those endless possibilities to a screeching halt when you allow yourself to give a negative meaning to an event. We live in a world of cause and effect. So there is always a consequence to our behavior.

Your behavior will always result in an outcome, which is the final step in this process. The outcome can be an event in itself, and then the cycle will continue. When you truly understand this concept, it is easy to see how people can repeatedly find themselves in the same types of relationships.

Let's look at the result of Patrice's self-talk. Later the next day James called me and gave me his perspective on what his girlfriend had done. At this point James was completely turned off by her insecurities. They had only been dating for a few months, and he couldn't stand the feeling of being on trial for a crime he did not commit.

I have always known James to be a very confident guy, and Patrice seemed to be a perfect match. Patrice was an executive for a pretty big company, and she gave off the appearance that she was full of confidence. However, now it was clear that her past was shaping her future.

They were on the verge of breaking up. Since I knew James loved Patrice, I decided to take them on as clients. I began to teach them this concept of taking control of their emotions. Within two months of practicing control, Patrice had finally found a way to stop putting her past in front of her. She finally broke the chain. She became a more positive person in every aspect of her life, not just in her relationship.

A relationship is made up of people, and some don't realize that, if you don't have the right people, you don't have the right relationship. When making an omelet with two eggs, I don't care how perfect one of them looks. If one egg is spoiled (rotten), the omelet will be ruined. The same rules apply to dating. You have to bring the best "you" possible to the table, or it will not work. I don't care how great a woman she is or how amazing he is. If you don't bring the best "you" to the table, the relationship is doomed.

Let's jump back into that leadership conference that changed my life. On my way home I got stuck in traffic, so I had plenty of time to wrap my mind around everything I had learned. Of course there were many topics that were taught to us, but, for some reason, only a few things replayed on my mental DVD player.

I remember blasting the heat in my car and it being a cold day outside, but I had put down the window a bit, allowing in the cool air to create the perfect balance. Then it happened out of nowhere. The thought infiltrated my mind, and it was loud and clear.

Being in a relationship is like being in traffic. All you can do is control what you do and hope for the best.

As I looked around me, some drivers seemed very annoyed by the congestion. You could see them speeding up and changing lanes, as if that was going to get them to their destination any faster. Some drivers were blowing their horns, frantically hoping that the cars would magically move out of their way.

Let me be the first to say, I am normally the most impatient person when it comes to traffic, but, for some reason that day, my spirit was calm. I was able to admire such a beautiful day, something I hadn't been able to do in months. Actually I felt a level of gratitude that I had never felt before. I knew it was because of what I was doing internally. I had started to truly control my self-talk. I was still very far from being where I needed to be, but I could feel my mental set point had started to move away from negative thinking.

This moment of epiphany helped me recall one of my favorite quotes from Tom Bodett, who states, "The difference between school and life? In school, you're taught a lesson and then given a test. In life, you're given a test that teaches you a lesson."

I had discovered something on my two-day trip. I had discovered a part of myself which I didn't know existed, and it felt amazing. I realized that I was the director, writer, and star of this movie called my life. I didn't have to audition, because I already had the part. I was not looking forward to the thoughts that would randomly appear in my mind, but I was prepared for them.

It was an unusually cold morning the next day. I left to go to work slightly earlier than normal because I wanted to get a head start on some of the projects I had been assigned. I needed to make a huge turnaround because it was obvious my work ethic had started to slip over the past few months. And then it happened. A song came on the radio, and the basic message in the song was "Your man can't do it like I can." I actually remember wanting to scream at the top of my lungs, "I can't believe she did that shit!" Before I could yell out that statement, I thought for a second. I actually stopped and said, "What does it mean?" For the first time I actually took a moment to change the meaning in my mind for everything that had happened.

Of course I could not change the past, but I didn't have to put the past in front of me either. This would be something I would have to do multiple times per day. In a matter of weeks I had finally found a way to stop erupting in anger. My girlfriend and I could now go out in public with our friends and not have the night ruined because of my behavior. It was as if I totally forgave her. At least that was the appearance.

The truth was, I hadn't fully forgiven her. I would think of her and Omar often. There was no way to stop myself from thinking about what had happened. There were times I would be in the middle of a meeting, and images of Tracy and Omar together would run through my mind.

It was as if I took on a second job to just control my emotions. All day, every day, I would have to challenge the meaning my mind wanted to automatically assign to the CRASH that was Tracy's infidelity. I was the only man I knew of who could take on the challenge of forgiveness to this degree. That became my reason; that became my "why."

I often thought to myself, what kind of man would I have to become in order to truly forgive? That was exciting to me, although it was difficult.

I had read about people who had become great as a result of a challenge they had to go through and to grow through. Now I was a sponge, constantly looking for something to absorb in order to become a better me. That "something" came in the form of reading books on dating, relationships, and marriage. It also came in the form of any book that had to do with personal development. I had to work on the habit of being myself.

There was one thing that confirmed to me that I was doing something special. Tracy and I were watching, in my opinion, one of the most romantic movies ever made, *The Notebook*. In the movie there is a scene which clearly demonstrates what true love could and should be.

I will never forget what happened next. Tracy turned to me with a sad but serious tone and said, "You are like Jesus." She didn't have to explain because I knew what she meant. She was basically implying that I was as forgiving as every story ever told about Jesus.

Before she made that statement, I felt a little crazy a lot of the time. Everyone around me thought I was stupid to remain in this relationship, and honestly I did too. The truth is I didn't forgive her until that point. It was like someone was recognizing me for my hard work and effort. Forgiveness became easier.

Can you see what that seminar did?

Before that class I could have easily had a different self-talk. "She is just saying that because she feels guilty." However that is not what I decided to do. I created a positive meaning. I told myself that I must be doing something great to almost bring her to tears by just being myself. This meaning would allow me to look forward to the next day.

With my self-talk, I justified staying with her, even though I didn't have to. Again I felt the responsibility of the people who called me, texted me, and emailed me so often. I had to show them how to handle a challenge, and, in return, I learned more than I had ever imagined. I realized I could change the way I saw anything. It was like magic. If I could change such a traumatic event, wouldn't it be possible to achieve wonders?

CHAPTER SUMMARY

- Events don't mean anything. Stop making up S*%! about them.

- Deciding who you want to be, and what different things and events mean, will not only help you to be the best "you" but also help you to find the right person and to keep the right person.

- No one has to know how bothered you were unless you want them to know.

- Changing what something means has an effect on how you feel. Now you control whether you have a positive or negative day.

- Finding love requires you to take your thoughts and emotions off autopilot.

What Were You Thinking???

Conscious vs. Subconscious Mind

H ere is the reason we set goals but don't accomplish
them.

You can say you want something and set a goal to hit
it, but that is a conscious decision. You are in control of
your conscious mind right now. To actually get what you
say you want and to accomplish that goal, it has to be a
subconscious decision. Your subconscious, or habits, run
your actions long-term.

Confused yet? Let me explain.

This is how your brain works. Let's just say you don't
believe you will find the perfect spouse. You may have had
several failed relationships, or all of the relationships
around you are dysfunctional. Since that is all you know, it
may be impossible for you to believe me when I say, "He
or she is on the way."

If I called you by your first name, you would respond
right away, because you hear your name every day. It has
actually become so much a part of you that it has now
moved from your conscious thoughts to the subconscious
mind. All that means is that recognizing your name is on

autopilot. You don't have to think consciously when you hear your name.

Think of the common habits in our society. A smoker doesn't have to be reminded to pull out a cigarette, because it is in his subconscious mind. A coffee drinker doesn't need to set an alarm when it is time to drink the next cup, because it is stuck in their subconscious. Knowing your name is a habit at this point. You don't have to consciously think it over.

Another example of this was when I was spending time with a friend of mine, who I had picked up earlier in the evening. As I was driving her back home, I saw the time was 5:00 a.m. I was so tired dropping her off that I didn't even remember getting back home. Driving home was a habit. My subconscious mind actually got me home, but I consciously wasn't awake.

This is the goal with life. The goal is to get your mind on autopilot when believing you will find love or to be successful. You control your thoughts. Positive thinking should become such a habit for you that it happens without you truly having to think about being positive.

One of the most important things I learned during the darkest emotional time in my life is that *thoughts become things*.

How does that apply to you?

Listen to me carefully. A good man or woman has to be in your hands long before he or she is in your hands. Let's just say that you don't have what you want in life right now. If you only operate on what you see, you will always get what you see. If you want more in your life, you may never get it if you can't see past where you are now.

Over the past few months my wife and I have noticed that there have been many trees cut down in the area. The other day I saw a lot of construction and plenty of signs around town that said New Home Construction. One day I drove by slow enough to pick up on what was happening, and I was blown away.

There were tents set up where they were giving people tours of houses that weren't even built yet. Huh? People were actually being sold on something that did not exist. These imaginary homes were upward of $500,000. I have been in sales for years, and it was sometimes difficult to get people to buy something they actually needed right away, never mind an imaginary home that wouldn't be up for at least a year.

All I'm trying to say is, you have to sell yourself on things that you want but are not here yet. In fact you have to sell yourself so well that you are willing to work extremely hard, all because you expect it to happen. Just like those prospective homebuyers committed their checkbooks because they expected the home will be there in a few months. It's not a hope or a wish. Trust me. They would not lay down that type of money unless they were sure.

I know the average person won't admit it, but most people see their major life goals as something they hope or wish they could achieve instead of something they know is definite.

This is why we so easily set New Year's resolutions but rarely follow through. It is amazing to see how many treadmills are running and elliptical machines are spinning in January. Two months later, the gym is empty. It's because people simply don't believe with conviction that they can reach their goal or that it's possible to achieve it. Their goal is still in their conscious mind and hasn't moved to their subconscious mind yet.

Again to make a measurable long-term change, it can't be just a conscious decision. It has to be a subconscious decision, which affects your habits. Here is an example of what most people are really thinking when they set a goal.

"I hope I find the love of my life, or I wish I could earn one million dollars."

The average person doesn't really believe they can achieve their goal. It is pretty much guaranteed that you will not achieve something that you do not believe you can achieve. The amazing thing is you could physically have everything you need to arrive at your goal, but your internal belief means everything in the equations of achievement.

Here is another example.

You may set a goal to go to work tomorrow morning as you do every morning. Now you have already been to work almost every day for an entire year. It's safe to say that it has become a habit for you. It's not like you set a goal to go to work tomorrow and you have to sit up late tonight trying to figure out how you are going to get there. By now you don't even have to think about it. You know the exact time you have to be in the car in order to get to work on schedule. You know exactly which road you will be taking, and you may even have a breakfast spot you always stop at. Going to work is a goal that you actually believe you can achieve and expect to.

How can you get some of your bigger goals, like being rich or finding your wife or husband, to be as simple and automatic as a smaller goal like tying your shoelaces?

I learned the following statement that would change the way my mind worked for the rest of my life.

Habits are thousands of times stronger than your desires.

You can desire to lose weight all you want. But that is a conscious decision and sounds good for a few hours, maybe a few days at most. However, your habits cause success and change, and your subconscious mind runs that part of your life. You will not take the actions necessary to accomplish what you say you want if your subconscious mind doesn't believe it. So if your habits are not in line with what you want, you will never get it. It's important to make a decision with your conscious mind regarding what your goals are and what you choose to believe. Then you have to systematically impress these beliefs into your subconscious until it becomes a habitual way of thinking.

Some people think "win" all the time, and some think the opposite all the time. There is some hope. Your brain has been created to do anything you want. It can be trained. We are all a product of our genes, and, if we do nothing to change how we are wired, we will maintain our perspectives, thoughts, ideas, and attitudes in our life, even if they don't lead us to happiness.

Think about how many years it has taken you to develop your current beliefs—eighteen, twenty, thirty-five, forty-two, fifty-one, sixty-eight?

How can you change years of training by accident or by luck?

You must purposely choose to change your life and your thinking. This isn't the lotto.

One of my favorite moments from the motion picture film *The Matrix* was when a question was posed to the protagonist. "Have you ever had a dream that was so real? What if you were unable to wake from that dream? How would you tell the difference between the dream world and the real world?"

Let's break it down. When you touch an ice cube, your fingers send a signal to the brain. The brain then gets the information and determines that you are touching something cold. So it sends a response back. Same with nightmares we remember upon waking, still feeling the fear, our heart still pounding fast and/or erratic.

So that quote from *The Matrix* actually has some truth to it. Your brain can't tell the difference between what is real and what isn't. The brain can't tell whether it's your senses or your imagination sending the signal, because, to the brain, they are both just electrical signals.

If you can imagine something with conviction, you can actually confuse the brain into thinking something is actually happening when in reality it's not. This is why you can't just hope something happens. You actually have to get into the feeling of already having what you say you want.

Words carry so much power that we have to be careful what we say, because we can speak it into existence.

My wife and I had our wedding in one of the most beautiful parts of Mexico. A few days before our trip, we were around a bunch of kids at a birthday party. I think that was where Zaida got sick. Her voice was starting to go, and she had flulike symptoms.

Since the wedding was only about four or five days away, we believed she would be fine by the wedding day. We had close to fifty family members and friends flying down to be a part of our ceremony. Since people were traveling from different parts of the country, everyone didn't arrive at the same time.

As soon as my grandmother landed in Mexico, she began to complain about severe back pain. Although she is eighty-eight years old, that has never been a major problem for her, so it worried me. Her physical frustration caused her to be annoyed, and it was affecting her interaction with us. She walked slowly back to her room in pain.

I felt bad that my grandmother, the eldest person on this trip, was enduring the most pain out of all of us. I couldn't have the woman who raised me be in so much pain on the greatest day of my life so far. I sat up for an hour that night praying and meditating.

I specifically prayed to take on my grandmother's pain. I felt that I was stronger than she was, and it would be better if I could take on her agony. Boy, was I wrong.

Although I was with my wife since she had become sick, her symptoms never transferred to me. I felt fine so far, but, for some reason, the next morning I felt worse than my wife. I couldn't swallow. My voice was gone completely. I couldn't believe it. I thought, maybe this is a coincidence.

The one thing that would prove to me that my illness didn't happen by chance was if my grandmother was feeling a little better. When my wife and I made it around the resort the next day, our family recognized how sick we were.

But, when I saw my grandmother, my first order of business was to see how she felt. I was blown away. She said she felt ten times better than she did the night before. Meanwhile I felt like crap.

In no way did I believe that I physically took my grandmother's pain from her. However, one of the things I learned from that event was, when you focus on something with a lot of passion and energy, you bring it into your life, if it is possible for you to imagine it.

It's possible I allowed myself to get sick. I really believed I could take on her pain. I felt it in my spirit that my thoughts would affect how she felt. How she felt had little to do with my thoughts and request. However, how I felt had everything to do with my belief.

The biggest lesson I learned was to be specific when I make a request. I had asked to take on my grandmother's pain, and I did just that. I could have easily asked to simply take away her pain. If I had, I might have avoided the unbearable pain in paradise. Then again maybe there was something poetic about my wife and me both having to use microphones to say our vows because we simply didn't have our voices back yet.

The brain is a powerful tool. What we think internally and then say out loud, it can manifest in the physical realm.

SETTING YOUR MENTAL SEARCH ENGINE TO "IDEAL MATE"

The Reticular Activating System (RAS) is a bunch of neural fibers at the base of the brain that filters and sorts the important from the less important information that the brain receives from your different senses. It is responsible for many things, such as controlling your muscle actions, breathing, sleep, wakefulness, and your focus. Every single moment it is filtering, trying to find the pieces of data that match with our habitual way of thinking.

The goal is to change the filter to focus and sort out as "important" the things that will help you accomplish your goals. Your RAS works like Bing or any search engine. As long as you program it with what you want, it will give you the results you put into it. It will find exactly what you need it to find and totally ignore what doesn't support the search inquiry.

If you type "Toyota" in the Bing search engine, will you get results for Michael Jackson? I'm almost certain you will not. Try it. If you have purchased a pair of shoes or some other item in the past, isn't it amazing how, before you owned that item, you may have only seen a few of them around? Shortly after you purchased those shoes, you start to see them in ads and you see ten people every day wearing them.

Suddenly an item that was far and few between is everywhere. Was it that those shoes didn't exist before you owned them? Or is it that you now notice them because it is in your mental search engine? I think you know the answer. Your search will only focus on what you tell it to, and it will ignore the rest.

The question to ask yourself, when wanting to be successful in love, is: what is in your search engine minute by minute, day by day?

Some people don't even realize that they have sabotaging topics in their mental search engine or their RAS. These same people then wonder why they keep seeing the same negative results.

You can push hard for a goal, but you will still miss all the little key factors or opportunities that would assist you in hitting that goal if your subconscious or RAS was programmed for what you don't want.

Let's say you have been cheated on by every guy you have ever been with; furthermore, you saw your father cheat on your mom growing up. Let's say now that "all men cheat" is the title in your search engine. Even if you have the greatest guy in the world, you will more than likely miss all of the little clues that support his commitment to you.

You will, on the other hand, happen to pick up on every letter in a text message, every word in overheard conversations that support the notion that he is a cheater. Your brain will literally ignore anything that doesn't coincide with the idea of him cheating on you.

While my wife and I were on vacation in the Dominican Republic, I witnessed firsthand what happens when you allow your search engine (RAS) to only pick up on behavior that supports your truth, even if it isn't a fact.

We met a couple who was enjoying their first vacation together. When they found out that I was a certified relationship coach, they began to ask me specific questions. That is when Rick explained how Diana had spoiled this surprise trip they were on.

One day Diana had come home, and, as soon as she had walked in the door, Rick had shut down his computer right away. In her mind, she had self-talk that probably told her that he was hiding something. According to the meaning she gave this event, only someone who was hiding something or cheating would have to be so secretive. Of course that self-talk conversation created a negative emotion.

The emotion, good or bad, always creates a behavior. In this case, her behavior was going through Rick's phone and computer when he wasn't looking. As a result of actions coming from her self-talk and resulting emotions, she eventually found out that he was being so secretive because he was trying to plan a trip for them to the Dominican Republic.

In this case, you can easily see what was in her RAS. Somewhere along the line she told herself the story that all men cheat. After speaking to her, it was clear that she had been cheated on in the past by someone she had really loved. If all men cheat, then any man had the potential to break her heart. I'm telling you, if you do nothing to change the story in your mind, you will always see the same results.

One thing you have to understand right now is, sometimes our ways of thinking have been drilled into our mind so deep that we don't realize that it is a part of our belief system or our story.

Here is one way to gauge how your RAS is programmed. Look at the results in your life right now. Your present day is a clear indication of what you are searching for subconsciously. Some people say that they are on a diet, and they want to lose pounds.

Unfortunately maybe they have this belief deep in their subconscious that diets never work, and there is really no way to be a certain weight unless your parents were around that size. Some people may have tried diets in the past, and they didn't lose anything.

So now maybe your subconscious mind causes you to focus on foods that will keep the weight on just to support your belief. Of course, this is not something these people are doing on purpose, but remember our subconscious is out of our direct control.

No matter what they say or try, unless they do the necessary work to change their RAS, their brains will find every bit of information to support that deep subconscious belief.

Take a second to imagine that you are in your car with all the intention in the world to make it to the nearest mall. You could be dressed for the mall; you have your coupons and all the money you need. So you hop in the car, and you turn on the GPS, expecting it will take you to the shopping mall. However, you fail to realize that your GPS is already set to home, and, until you program in the desired address (which in this case is the mall), the GPS will not change its direction to take you to the mall.

The bad news is programing yourself doesn't usually happen as fast as programing a GPS. The great news is, once your RAS is programed to find what you want, it will work just like a GPS. Notice your GPS has thousands of streets and turns programmed into it, but it doesn't bombard you with all that useless information. In other words, it actually ignores hundreds of thousands of streets and only focuses on the information and streets that will take you to the mall.

Even if everything is lining up and the best guy possible arrives in your life, your RAS could filter it out as unimportant and won't notify your conscious brain. If you only see what you don't want, then that is exactly what you will keep finding, because it is in your search engine.

When you are focused on how bad your last relationship was or how unsuccessful you have been with men or women in the past, you will keep finding things to support that. This becomes a habit of what your subconscious will look for: things to reinforce that belief—like overheard conversations, news articles, random memories, television, etc.

Think of the example in the last chapter when Patrice automatically jumped to the thought that James was cheating on her. James is the guy she has been praying for, but she misses all the opportunities that would confirm that. Her RAS has been set on cheating men, so of course her self-talk will reflect what is in her search engine.

I know a young man named David who had seemingly found his ideal spouse. She was perfect for him from the outside looking in. Unfortunately he had a belief that relationships never last when they start out strong, because people get comfortable. I remember him saying that years ago, and I didn't really know how much he believed it, until our mutual friends and I watched him drive away this woman.

All of his actions were totally in line with this belief. At one point in their relationship, he said, "Trevor, she doesn't cook as much as she did in the beginning." It was amazing that all of his friends, including myself, had noticed that she had taken on a new position at work which caused her to get home later than normal. I honestly think David didn't even realize.

They eventually broke up, and here we are years later, and he is still saying how much he misses her. Unfortunately for him, she is now married with children. He didn't even realize that he had sabotaged that great relationship because of something he didn't even know he was focused on.

After observing many people argue, I have found that most people get caught up on one insignificant issue that has little relevance to the core disagreement. However, what seems insignificant to you and me is something that their RAS has singled out as important and in line with their beliefs. Remember beliefs (our habitual way of thinking) and habits in general are thousands times stronger than desires or wants.

If you believe it is hard to find your ideal spouse, then guess what? It will be. You have to learn how to focus on what you want. It is hard to change the world around you, unless you change the world within you. It is best to focus on the solution and not the problem.

UPLOADING DEFAULT/FACTORY SETTINGS

It usually takes around thirty days of constant activity to make it a habit. To be safe let's just say ninety days.

Have you ever let the steering wheel go while driving and notice, after a short period of time, how the car drifts in one direction? We have to understand that our thoughts usually have their own agenda. Just like when you are behind the wheel of a car and need to help steer it, you have to gain a little control over your thinking. If not, you may find yourself in love's ditch.

This is where having a "workout" partner pays off. You want someone who can hold you accountable. This is yet another reason why coaching is so important.

You have all the power and all the control when it comes to your thinking. As we discussed in Stop Making Up S*%!, it is your self-talk that determines how you will behave and ultimately handle the situation.

This reminds me of when my wife had a small party at our home on a spring evening. Once people started to arrive, I knew the temperature in the house would start to rise. There was an evening breeze outside that would cool the temperature down, so it didn't quite make sense to turn on the AC when I could just open up the house.

After about an hour, I noticed the temperature hadn't really changed much. I had opened the door, expecting the room to cool down. Everyone was having a great time playing Taboo, but the room still didn't cool down. Finally I just happened to hear the sound of the heating system running. Duh! I realized I still had the heat on.

The reason the heat didn't activate for the past week was because I had the temperature set at seventy-five degrees, and the natural temperature in the house was seventy-five degrees. Now when I opened the door to make it cooler inside, the heat was kicking in to keep the house at seventy-five or above. Since the music was so loud, I didn't realize the heat was on and working against the cooler temperature I was trying to create.

Although I had a goal of a cool house, my thermostat had a job to do, and it was doing it very efficiently. There is something in the brain that operates the same way as your house thermostat, and it is called the psycho-cybernetic mechanism, or PCM.

The PCM is designed to control certain specifications and make necessary changes to any deviation from its original set point. As human beings, we all have a set point called our "comfort zone." No matter how bad we want to change so that we can meet our goal, just keep in mind that there is something working to keep things the way they are now.

In the example of my house, the system picked up on the cool air coming in, and it started sending hot air to get the temperature back to seventy-five degrees. The PCM will pick up on any major diversion from your comfort zone set point and will send the necessary information to your nervous system to take the appropriate action.

Your nervous system will then initiate an emotional catalyst to amend the disparity and bring you back to your comfort zone. This entire process happens automatically. It also happens so fast that you won't even notice it. This is usually the point where you start to feel doubt. I hear people say things like "This stuff isn't working." People may feel fear and anxiety as well.

"I'm not sure I can do this."

These are all things that people say out loud or to themselves when going for a goal that will stretch them.

When I became single after my last relationship, I moved into my own apartment, and I decided to go a year without television. Funny thing is, early on I often felt this overwhelming desire to drive down the street to my aunt's house to watch her TV when a particular program was being aired.

My reason for not watching TV was to monitor its influences on my life, and here I was doing everything possible to still find a way to indulge in the experience of the idiot box. I believe it was my psycho-cybernetic mechanisms trying to justify why it was okay to pay my aunt a visit for the wrong purpose.

The reason I was successful with this endeavor was because I purposely didn't have cable. I don't think I would have had the discipline to leave the TV off if I had had the option to turn it on at my house. Sometimes you have to completely take yourself out of an environment.

Some of you may say, "Why did you find it necessary to eliminate television?"

Remember we are affected by what we see, hear, and experience. Best-selling author and psychologist Denis Waitley eluded to the fact that TV and advertising could potentially affect us in a similar way in which secondhand smoke affects the nonsmoker.

Just think about that for a minute.

There have been many people who have developed lung cancer even though they weren't the ones smoking.

They were just in the vicinity long enough with a person who did smoke. What if television affected us in the way secondhand smoke can? You don't have to be the only ones cheating, being lazy, gender bashing, and voicing how hard relationships are, or screaming how all men are dogs or all women want to do is spend money.

Just think about the many commercials you see on a daily basis. If they had no effect on you whatsoever, why would companies spend so much money to advertise using them? During the Super Bowl, companies fight for digital real estate because they know that millions of people will be watching that event.

Some companies will spend over one million dollars for a thirty- to sixty-second spot. Don't you think they have done enough research beforehand on how advertising will get you to buy their product? That is why your favorite bag of chips or most popular beer will shell out millions for a Super Bowl ad. It is because they know those ads work.

Now you understand why it is so hard to make the necessary changes to attract success in any area of your life. Maybe you already knew this, but just didn't know how to change it. There are many things that can be done, but one thing is for sure. As said by Jim Rohn, "Finding is reserved for the people who are searching."

If you start looking for the different ways to change your RAS and your PCM, you are guaranteed to find the positive search results. Part of the reason I wrote this book was to get you to start or to improve your journey to greatness.

While traveling on that road to greatness, it is important to guard the media influences you allow to penetrate your subconscious mind.

MONITOR WHAT INFLUENCES YOUR SELF-TALK

Years ago, Omar (who I've acquainted you with in earlier chapters) told me about the time he went to a retreat at a well-known billionaire's home. This gentleman owned several companies and was responsible for many inventions. During some downtime at the retreat, a few guys began to tell this billionaire a dirty joke.

When the billionaire realized that the joke contained profanity, he immediately interrupted them before they could finish. Everyone was confused as to why their host didn't want to hear the punch line of the seemingly harmless joke. He said, "I'm sorry. I can't listen to the rest of that joke, because, once it goes into my mind, I can't control it."

What he was really saying is that something as simple as a joke has the potential to become a part of who you are. Maybe you don't want to be a billionaire, so you don't have to evaluate every single thing you hear. It's very possible that you don't ever want to be a millionaire so you don't have to eliminate everything that you see. You may, however, want to become the best "you" possible to attract your ideal mate, so it can't hurt to monitor the things you see and hear.

You will read this statement about monitoring what you see and hear a few times because I really want you to consider your own version of this. If you are already in a relationship that is not in your best interest, this may not be easy.

When I left my five-year relationship with Tracy, I was living on my own. I decided that I would not sign up for cable when I first moved into my bachelor pad. I had this idea of going without television for ninety days. By the time ninety days had rolled around, I realized a drastic difference in myself.

Then I said I would do another ninety days. I actually went a year without television. I filled my time with reading books, listening to audiobooks, and watching different lectures. The majority of my four to six discretionary hours went to personal growth and hanging out with different lady friends.

By the time the average person handles the necessities of life—such as sleeping, commuting to and from work, and actually working—he or she is usually left with three to five hours of free time. We all fill that time with something, and for most people there is something magnetic about that wonderful invention called TV.

I wanted to see the Miami Heat play on ESPN one day, so I went to my aunt's house, which was about ten minutes away, early on in my ninety-day run. It was my PCM trying to get me back to my comfort zone.

I tried to justify why going there to watch the game made sense. I laughed it off because it wasn't a big deal as long as I continued to pour more good into my brain than bad. I would watch less than an hour of TV every week. By sticking to my ninety-day TV detox, I was able to control the messages put in front of me.

Below are some of the other life lessons to help keep my RAS in check. Through daily affirmations, being cautious of my associations, and taking time to dive into personal development/coaching, and prayer, I was able to program the right advertisements in my mind and not the toxic ones.

FOCUS, FOCUS, FOCUS

My father always told me, "You are going to be like the people you hang around." I never really understood what he meant until college graduation day. I was sitting outside on the lawn near our campus pond. I looked around and noticed that most of the people I hung around with were graduating alongside me after our five years. If I had hung around instead with the kids on the three-year-graduation plan, like my father had suggested, I may have graduated in three years.

A general rule to follow is, if you hang around five broke people, you will be number six. If you hang around five rich people, you will be number six. If you hang around five attractive people, well, that may not always work, but I'm sure you understand my point.

When it comes to associations, you have to decide which category someone needs to fit into if necessary. There are people who may require you to limit the amount of time you spend with them because of their negative influence. If this person is family, be careful to not cut them off completely. There will be some people who you have to eliminate from your life altogether, because they are holding you back.

In contrast, there are some people who are great influences and who you will have to increase your time with. Their overall outlook and energy will rub off on you in such a positive way that you will desire to be around them more, just so you can see who you become. In fact reading this book is like hanging with me while I challenge you to think bigger.

A great suggestion is to find someone who has a similar goal to yours and make sure you push each other toward that goal every chance you get. Part of being a good "workout" partner is to always work on yourself first. After all, who you are and who you develop yourself to be will have either a negative or positive effect on your partner.

I don't care what your day looks like. There is nothing that should get in the way of you reading ten pages of a good book or listening to fifteen minutes of a good audiobook every day. It's your chance to be around some of the most profound and influential people. Remember what you do in your personal time shapes your life. You are in more control over your life and your results than you think.

Having a coach was by far the most important thing I did to start my quantum leap. Working with a marriage counselor caused me to think bigger. This is the primary reason I became a certified coach. I wanted to be to others what my teachers were to me.

No matter what you believe, there seems to be a positive effect when we connect to our source. There are several ways to accomplish this task. Two popular ways are prayer and/or meditation. I would meditate and pray almost every night, and it is something I still practice today.

CHAPTER SUMMARY

- Your habitual way of thinking got you the life you see today.

- Constantly bombard yourself with the things and people who cause you to focus on getting what you say you want.

- When looking to find love or to make the most amazing relationship work, it must be expected, not hoped for. Start expecting to find answers and the instructions to what you want.

- The Law of Attraction uses the law of your brain. Keep in mind that there will often be a pull to return to your comfort zone. Fight back!

LIGHTS, CAMERA, ACTION

DIRECTING YOUR FAIRY TALE

You have complete control in finding your ideal mate. In the book *Think and Grow Rich*, Napoleon Hill describes the thirty causes of failure after researching and interviewing some of the most financially successful people in our history.

One of the items (number fifteen) was on the topic of choosing the wrong partner for marriage. Hill concluded that marrying the wrong spouse is the:

> ...most common cause of failure. The relationship of marriage brings people intimately into contact. Unless this relationship is harmonious, failure is likely to follow. Moreover, it will be a form of failure that is marked by misery and unhappiness, destroying all signs of AMBITION. [Emphasis added.]

I find it interesting that number fifteen is in the middle of the list. So you say to yourself, "No problem. I will just focus on finding the right woman, and I will find her." The Law of Attraction is amazing, but it truly means nothing without the Law of Action. You can want something really bad. It could even be something that was meant for you to have. But without the Law of Action—getting up and doing something to get it—your chances of actually getting what you desire drop by 99.978 percent.

I heard one of my favorite artists say, "Luck is not some mystical energy that dances around the universe randomly bestowing people with satisfaction and joy."

You create your own luck. How do you do this? The key is to constantly grow and become a better "you" so that, when opportunity presents itself, you are ready. When the things you desire begin to manifest in your life due to you taking action, some people will refer to you as being lucky. However, it is your methodical study and repetition of thinking bigger, and more positively, that caused your greatness.

Here is the big question.

What actions should you take when it comes to finding love for yourself?

I believe you have that answer buried inside you, but you need certain information, combined with your life experiences, to create your life as you see fit. This is why they have coaches in sports. It is hard to see the whole court or the field when you are on it.

This next concept is one of the easiest ideas to grasp but can also be one of the most difficult things to find. However, it is possible. The goal is to find someone who wants to and can meet your needs as much as you want to and can meet that person's needs.

Michael Jordan would practice so much that it became routine to perform at a high level. Obviously his approach to the game of basketball has been a successful one. Many times we have watched Michael Jordan win many games in those crucial moments, when only a great play would win the game. In various interviews, he stated that the reason he was able to rise to the occasion is because he has been in a similar moment during practice. He has rehearsed this moment not only physically but mentally as well. He had practiced certain moves so often that he no longer has to try to make a play; it becomes automatic.

Here is the one thing you have to understand. Michael Jordan will tell you that he has been in many situations where he was unable to make the great play to win the game. However, we remember his greatness because of the times he was successful. You no longer have to live your life based on your failures. They were only there to make you great.

This is what you want to do in your love life. Sure, you won't get every situation right, but you will often succeed because you have now made winning a habit. When certain situations arise, you will have pride in knowing it won't require a large amount of thinking, because that won't allow you to enjoy the process.

It would be great if you can be natural and let things unfold with confidence because your natural action is subconsciously an informed one. It would be wise to study the things that will allow you to find and keep your ideal partner.

When the time comes, you can rely on your gut feeling, because you have put yourself in the best possible position. I remember listening to a sermon in church one day, and the topic was a verse in Proverbs, Chapter 24 (NIV). The verse stated:

[3] By wisdom a house is built, and through understanding it is established;

[4] through knowledge its rooms are filled with rare and beautiful treasures.

The true message is in the simplicity of this verse. Wikipedia defines **Wisdom** as "a deep understanding and realization of people, things, events, or situations, resulting in the ability to apply perceptions, judgments, and actions in keeping with this understanding."

Wisdom seems to be your ability to apply everything you have learned. Wikipedia also defines **Knowledge** as "a familiarity with someone or something, which can include facts, information, descriptions, or skills acquired through experience or education." **Understanding** is defined as "a psychological process related to an abstract or physical object, such as a person, situation, or message whereby one is able to think about it and use concepts to deal adequately with that object."

You can build your house on love, but it has to be built with wisdom. Most people never think about how important knowledge is when regarding love. They focus so much on how they feel, they never really understand that their failure in love comes from their lack of knowing, not necessarily lack of feelings.

Those facts, information, descriptions have been given to us by television, music, and movies. And our lives are on autopilot based on the things we know. Since no one really takes the time to teach us about finding true love, and we spend no time searching for answers, we use those bits and pieces of information from media as a guide.

First, we must get the knowledge and then understand it. However, the ultimate test is if we can apply it to our life. That is where true wisdom is defined.

The people we watch in movies, on TV, or see in magazines haven't studied love either. So in essence we emulate failures as they fail. There has never been a more accurate time to use the phrase "the blind leading the blind." So why is it that we leave something so important to influences that only have a purpose of entertaining and not educating? How can we expect these things to really educate us?

We want to experience lifelong love, but we give little attention to learning about it. Of course we don't watch movies and TV for education. However, whatever goes into our brain from any of our senses is what mixes with our decision-making process. So instead of looking for wisdom and knowledge on how to love, we end up seeking long walks in the park, nice round butts, tall and handsome, big breasts, hand-holding, passionate kisses, etc. Of course these are all the images we see on a daily basis.

When we sit in a movie theater to watch our favorite movie, we rarely think of everything that goes into it, such as how long the writers spent creating the story or about each actor studying his or her part. Some actors have to spend months on very strict diets to change their bodies. It never occurs to most people that there is an enormous amount of time and money that goes into equipment, like cameras, lights, props, and many other things which make a blockbuster.

Just like there is a purposeful process to create a great movie, there is a method to creating an incredible love story.

In our own lives I think most people forget or never realize they are the director of their own movie. Yes, your life is a movie. Of course there are a few small differences, like duration. There are also some similarities, like the need to improvise at times. The average movie is under three hours, but your life may last one hundred years. Of course in the movies they summarize all those years and just tell the details that make the story interesting.

Here are a few interesting things about this movie called your life story.

The first thing is that your story wouldn't be very interesting if everything was perfect. I want you to think of your favorite movie of all time. Let me ask you a question.

119

Was there any drama, despair, pain, difficulty, any kind of transition in the story line?

Of course there was. It wouldn't be very interesting if it didn't have some sort of change involved. I can't imagine a movie going from start to finish where everything was fine for the entire film. With that said, just take a second to embrace all of the challenges and bad things that have happened in your life. All it does is make your movie interesting. Also keep in mind that we are both the writers and the actors in this film called life as well.

It's important that we, as the writers, make sure our story doesn't stay focused on the challenges. Once you grasp this concept, you will realize that there is nothing in your life that can't be changed. You must first understand that you have the power.

What power am I speaking of? Please allow me to explain.

USING YOUR POWER

I have heard many times that we have been created in the image of our Creator. That is a powerful statement. That would mean that you are like a GOD. I did not say that you were God. What I did say is you have qualities like the Creator. If that is the case, then believing that you are the director of your life should seem very believable now.

Years ago I was preparing one night for a seminar I would be presenting the next day, and I felt so much pressure, because I would be in front of a huge crowd. I had less than fifteen hours to come up with a training program that would truly blow away my audience.

While I was typing up the gathered information I was going to share, I came across a news article. There was a story of a ninety-year-old woman who found the strength to lift a car off of her grandson who was trapped underneath. If you are like me, you are probably wondering how a ninety-year-old woman could lift such a heavy object. Did she get anointed with some magical power right there on the spot? I believe that she had that power inside her all along. She just needed something to help her bring it out of her.

In this case her adrenaline was flowing, and she didn't want her grandson to die. What about those stories of the placebo effect? I have heard of doctors giving patients a pill made of sugar but telling them it is the cure for a particular illness. As a result the patient takes the pill and no longer has the illness, even though they were just given sugar and not an actual cure. What this means it that they somehow miraculously healed themselves. They just believed so much that the pill would cure them that they actually healed themselves.

Some people would look at these events and think, it's a miracle. I see things like this and wonder how we can harness this power without having to have an outside stimulus. Sometimes when I stay up too late, I see these infomercials where a preacher will lay his or her hands on someone in an effort to cure them. Within moments that person starts to feel better as if his or her body was taken over. That power was already inside them, because God, or our Creator, is in everything He creates.

Of course this is an extreme example, but my only point is to illustrate to you that you have more power inside you than you think. Your Creator created you for greatness, but the world has programmed you to fail.

Someone who is serious about a lifelong relationship would have to take the time to create love as they see fit. If you are over the age of eighteen, I'm sure you have had the luxury of having someone fall for you or have a crush on you. If you have been denied such an experience, let me paint the picture for you.

Everything you do, everything you say somehow has a positive effect on that person. In most cases we have no clue what we are doing to make this person feel this way. It is like the old cartoon where the skunk is attracted to the cat. The cat has no clue why the skunk wants the cat so desperately.

However, in just being itself, the cat emits a certain power that can only increase its self-confidence. After all, if someone can see us in such a high light, we must be awesome. Having someone admire you in such a way sometimes can be the ultimate confidence booster.

Although you can rely on naturally attracting someone in this manner, I suggest you take on the role of being the writer/director/actor in this movie called life.

Sure, you could play the part of the viewer and just sit in the audience of your life, but why leave such an important task to chance? With that said, you have to realize that there is no room for improvising or leaving your life to chance.

What that means is you must always make sure you are working on personal development. In fact your main job should be to bring the best version of you to the table. Throughout this book, we have discussed different things you can do to make yourself a better person. Remember, once you understand that love is an action more than a feeling, a verb more so than a noun, you will understand that true love involves a level of strategy.

WHO AND HOW TO CHOOSE

Let go of this crazy idea that true love and passionate romance is this magical world where everything will just fall in place if things are meant to be. It is possible that, if you believe this, you may grow very old waiting for the Tetris pieces of your life to align. Television, music, and movies make this magical appearance of love seem romantic, but it is just a cover-up for our laziness.

Showing people how much they are worth by putting forth effort is part of what creates seduction. Leaving things to chance is a recipe for disaster, and shows that you don't take love and romance very seriously.

Falling in love is more about psychology than magic. Sure, there may be a person designed specifically for you. If this is true, I can only imagine it is like any other gift from God. When you don't work to cultivate it, you will only lose it. This is why dating effectively is important.

Keep this in mind: experienced hunters set their traps long before their prey comes into the picture. I was watching a show on how they catch lobsters with these huge traps. The fishermen spent all day going to different locations where they had laid traps to pick up their lobsters. They must have had a dozen traps in different parts of the water, but the most amazing thing is that they had set the traps days before they actually picked up their catch.

Since this is your movie, it would be wise to only audition key people for the supporting role. I'm sure Steven Spielberg has plenty of actors and actresses who he believes are great. However, I'm sure, when he has a specific movie he is working on, only a few of those people would even fit a particular role. Basically every great actor/actress isn't right for every role. Some of my past girlfriends were and still are amazing "actresses" in the movie of my life, but they just didn't fit the role of my future wife like Zaida does.

One of the most important things you can do to create the fairy tale called your love is to find someone with similar values to yours. Sometimes people choose the highest mountain to climb. Although setting high goals can be an amazing thing in other areas of life, when it comes to love and finding your ideal spouse, you will have a much more enjoyable experience if you share a lot in common as to key principles.

This doesn't mean that you have to find someone who is exactly like you. There is no one in the world just like you. Just think about this. There isn't a person in the world who has been around you every day of your life but you. You were there when you were dancing as hard as you could in the mirror to that Beyoncé song. You were there when you played basketball in the backyard by yourself and imagined you were Michael Jordan.

Pick your battles wisely. Some people simply have not found their ideal spouse because they constantly go after the people who are not that into them. Just because you had great sex doesn't mean they care for you like you care for them.

Choose people who naturally respond to you the way you feel your future husband or wife would. That is of course assuming that you want your potential partner to reciprocate the love you are giving them. If they don't respond to you naturally, you can still have a good time with them if you choose. However, please take them off the list as a potential lifelong partner.

I know life is all about the challenge, but it is not a great feeling to chase someone for the rest of your life if they don't desire you equally. I'm here to tell you that there is someone out there who wants you as much as you will want them. That makes your job easier. Save yourself the headache and the heartache.

Remember you are casting for this movie called your life. It is crucial that you consider selecting someone who has a natural quality that attracts you. What the quality is really depends on you. It could be the way they walk, the way they talk, their character. It could be their passion for the church or their passion for guns. It could even be their style but, whatever the attribute is, make sure it is something that is attractive to you.

Those attributes will inspire an emotion in you, and that emotion will be part of the fuel you will need to actively show them love. Remember, if love is an action, you want something to initially push you to do what it takes to possibly meet this person's needs.

When you have more energy, you are more creative and excited to express love. For me the initial things were how beautiful my future wife was, and the fact that I had met her years ago in college. Those two things made it easy for me to at least consider her as my potential wife and take the necessary steps to go further.

Keep in mind, long-term love is best when a decision to love that person is the driving force for being with that person. Even though I thought my wife was drop-dead gorgeous, I knew that I couldn't base my love for her on that, because looks can fade.

I also knew that, for me to pursue a woman for lifelong love, I needed her to be physically amazing. If not, I felt that my attentions would be easily stolen by the first beautiful woman who crossed my path.

126

I additionally liked the idea of having met her in the past, and now she gets to meet this well-put-together version of me. I dated with confidence and no pressure, because I knew who I was, and I knew what type of woman I wanted. My blueprint was crystal clear to me.

When it comes to evaluating emotions, you also want to pay close attention to your effect on them. You want to make sure that this potential lover responds to you the right way. Of course, the right way is subjective to whoever is doing the evaluating. You could be wasting your time if that person doesn't demonstrate how he or she is into you emotionally.

You want there to be something about you that has sparked an emotional response in them as well. That emotion is part of what makes you potentially their ideal partner.

It is important not to spend too much time trying to interpret what he or she is thinking or doing. I come across women all the time who do their best to create an explanation for why their man doesn't align with her lifelong love blueprint. You should be more focused on finding someone who aligns with who you are and what you want out of life rather than spending time with that person who isn't a good fit for you.

This is part of why knowing who you are and what you want from love is so important. If you have an idea of what your love blueprint is, it makes it easier to walk away when what is in front of you doesn't match up. You could waste your lifetime trying to figure out why some people are the way they are.

One of the things you can pay attention to is the responses that are not usually controlled, such as a smile, a blush, or maybe even them raising their voice. Also the bad/good habits they demonstrate every day. One way you can do this is to find a way to observe them in their natural habitat. Of course they will more than likely be performing when they are around you.

How do they behave when they are around their friends?

One thing I heard my wife say was that she had observed my behavior when I was around my family. She watched the way I would treat the three women who raised me, my grandmother and two aunts. I also did the same thing. I watched Zaida around her friends. I also looked at pictures of her when she was younger, to get an idea of what has contributed to the woman who was standing in front of me.

So ask yourself, do they text you back when you call them? Are you okay with that? Again you will have a much more enjoyable time dating if you keep your attention on people who naturally respond in the way that is most desirable for you. Remember we already discussed that you need more than physical attraction to make the relationship last.

You have to decide if they are showing you the attention emotionally that you need to feel comfortable. By this time, you understand the importance of being complete before you meet someone; that way you aren't looking for them to make you happy.

You are also creating an environment for the right situation to flourish. You are prepping the soil for the greatest tree ever planted. Think of all the trees that have come from one tree. The fruit on the tree has seeds in it, so once the fruit hits the ground, new seeds are being planted indirectly which will create another tree.

Your love (development of new seeds) will lead to a different/better world (seeds that were harvested and grew into more new trees).

Keep in mind that if your prospective partner has a quality that strongly contradicts who you are as a person, it may be wise to evaluate if it is a deal breaker. No one can tell you what your deal breakers are. It is really up to you to decide what is important for you when it comes to long-term love and whether a certain person is in line with that.

It is important to find someone who has similar ideas, interest, and habits as you. It's crucial to evaluate if they have similar beliefs on what a relationship should be. If you both are not on the same page regarding life's major issues, then your words and actions will conflict with their being (which they have spent years building). We have to spend time entering his or her spirit. You want to see the world through his or her eyes. What if it was possible to find someone who you don't have to argue with ever?

You can really get people out of their shell if you become more like them. A mirror image of them is one way to feed their ego. But if you have to pretend to be like them, you may end up living a miserable life. I would hate to be successful at being someone else.

Doesn't it make sense to just find someone who is similar to you?

If you disagree on certain issues, make sure it's something you don't have a challenge adapting to or accepting. There is nothing more pleasing than having someone who is comfortable being with you—the real you. We all love ourselves, and it is a great thing to be with someone who has similar ideals and tastes.

This validates us in a strange way. It confirms to us that all of our life decisions were good ones. This goes for your partner as well. Your self-esteem would be somewhat threatened if your partner was completely different from you. You have spent twenty, thirty, forty-plus years building habits. It won't feel good to have someone come along and contradict them as if you were totally wrong all those years.

EQUITY AND BALANCE WHEN IT COMES TO RELATIONSHIPS

After recently going through the house-hunting process, I realize that it is a very tedious game of shopping for the best features and the best price. I thought maybe I was wrong for reducing looking for ideal love to that of shopping for the best deal on a house, until I started to research the topic and realized that there have been many studies on the subject.

When it comes to shopping for a home, these are a few things we specifically looked for.

The first thing was location. Zaida could not stand the thought of going back to living in a certain neighborhood. She thought simply, if our parents had worked so hard to get us to the point where we are now, it is our responsibility to take life and our children to the next level.

We were looking at one house in particular. The Realtor had sent us pictures of it, and everything seemed fine, so we decided to meet her at the house. While we were driving through the surrounding neighborhood, I could see her reaction all over my wife's face. She had the look of someone who had just taken a double shot of straight lime juice. When we finally arrived on the street where the house was, we noticed the straw that broke the camel's back.

There was a group of men standing outside drinking beer. No, there wasn't a barbecue going on. No, there wasn't a party going on inside the house, and the men had stepped outside to get away from the women. They just thought it was okay to stand outside. Needless to say, my wife drove right by the house.

Aside from the location, the other thing we wanted was to make sure the size of the bedrooms was reasonable. Some of the houses appeared to be no bigger than a really big closet. So my wife said we have to eliminate those from our list. We also needed decent-size bathrooms. After looking through a few homes, we realized the bathrooms were way too small for her liking.

Of course those houses were eliminated from our list as well. There were a few things we absolutely could not compromise on, and there were a few things we knew that we could fix and customize the way we saw fit. We had a list of things we absolutely needed in our ideal house.

I discovered something called the equity theory by behavioral psychologist John Stacey Adams. Wikipedia defines it as "a theory that attempts to explain relational satisfaction in terms of perceptions of fair/unfair distributions of resources within interpersonal relationships." According to some studies, most relationships would have a better chance of longevity if they were equal in what they bring to the table. People want to feel like they are getting a great deal.

Motivational speaker Jim Rohn says, "Success is something you attract by the person you become."

I don't think this is any different when it comes to relationships. So it is wise to become what you want in a lover. A relationship seems more likely to proceed to marriage if it is equitable, according to best-selling author Leil Lowndes.

Shopping for an equitable spouse is shopping for an ideal spouse. Now when I say "ideal" spouse (or "ideal" house), that doesn't mean perfect; it is more like "perfect for you." When it comes to love and relationships, the equity principle suggest that no one wants to feel like they are putting in more love or energy than the other partner. If there is a huge imbalance, one partner will more than likely become emotionally frustrated and start to feel shortchanged.

On the other hand, if one person believes they are getting more than they deserve in the relationship, they will also become emotionally frustrated. In other words, finding balance in a relationship is a worthy goal. Keep in mind you don't have to be exactly the same on each one. You and your mate may be great in different areas, which may help you balance out the equation. Some of the most common balancing factors people focus on are:

- appearance,
- money,
- reputation,
- social status,
- knowledge,
- character.

When we look at couples like Angelina Jolie and Brad Pitt, we can agree that they are on the same level as far as their physical appearance. I'm not saying a relationship should be based on looks. What I am saying is that, if two people are equitable, it is less likely that Angelina will look at Brad and think to herself, "I can do much better." It is also less likely that Brad will feel insecure because he knows deep down he can measure up to his superstar-actress partner.

I'm sure you have seen or have been in a relationship where one partner was clearly more attractive than the other. Oftentimes if you talk to that couple, you will realize that the less attractive partner is very insecure and always filled with a sense of worry, doubt, and fear. That person may not even voice this to anyone, but studies show that he or she becomes miserable, and it is all because, in their mind, they didn't measure up. In other cases, the more attractive partner realizes the disparity, and they start to feel like they can do better after that initial rush of euphoria settles.

If you want long-lasting love, it is better to find someone on your level. If you are not sure, get an unbiased opinion from someone you trust. Your thoughts affect how you approach life and ultimately how others perceive you because we are such a visual society. However, a truly confident person can cancel out this theory if they are confident enough.

It is also possible for the less attractive partner to be superior in another areas which may cause a balance in the relationship but don't bank on that. You should never have feelings of not measuring up to the attractiveness of your partner. Even if this is true, that type of mentality can often be the demise of a budding relationship.

Similar to physical appearances, you may want to find someone who is financially similar. Now if they make more than you, that's fine. However, if they are a multimillionaire and you make thirty thousand dollars per year, it may not work. Again these are not rules, and it depends on your confidence level.

Studies have shown that you can go after the dream spouse who earns a significantly larger amount of money than you, but usually the relationships that progress to marriage and remain successful are the ones where each person's income is more balanced. The money imbalance is something that seems to mess with the mind in the long run. Again the simple advice here is to become like the person you want to attract.

In an inequitable relationship moneywise, you may start to feel like you don't have a voice when it comes to certain bills, since you didn't bring home much money. I have seen many couples struggle with this because one spouse paid all the bills and the other spouse felt insecure.

Unless you are strong in other areas, you may really start to think that you are not needed and that your partner can do things without you. On the other hand, since he or she is a multimillionaire, there may come a time when that person feels like you are just with him or her for the money, and maybe he or she can do better, since you can't really relate to the effort it takes to be where your partner is financially.

I remember when I first started dating my future wife. I had noticed a book on her coffee table. I don't remember the title, but it had something to do with money affecting your choice of a spouse. It told a story of how money affects love in a relationship. At that moment, I realized she was conscious of how her potential man's finances would impact her life and vice versa.

I have seen plenty of couples who are not on the same page when it comes to money. One person is a big spender, and the other is a big saver. No matter where you are moneywise at this point, just make sure you are doing everything you can do to ensure your finances are in the best possible state before you find your partner.

Once I started living on my own, I made a few decisions which have impacted my life. I spoke to two gentlemen who had achieved a certain level of prestige when it came to finances. I wanted to know what a great savings plan was. I know the common suggestion is to save at least 10 percent of your income, but these two gentlemen saved more than that. Although their answers were slightly different, it was apparent that I should save at least 30–60 percent.

Now I'm not saying that this is something you should do. What I am saying is to have some sort of plan. Men especially need to focus on that because you never know when you will meet the love of your life. It will not be a good feeling to want to marry a woman but yet can't afford to buy her a ring. There are plenty of reasons to have a good savings plan, and there are also several sources to learn how to do better when it comes to the green stuff. You don't have to be rich. Just know that you may be judged on your earning potential.

Another habit I picked up while I was single was to turn off the TV, to cancel the cable. Since I didn't have a need to watch television anymore, I was able to avoid a cable bill. If you study success when it comes to money, you will realize there are a few good rules to follow. Keep this phrase in mind: *It's not how much you make but how much you keep that counts.*

So you should keep this in mind when evaluating a spouse. It may be an easier life if you are with someone who believes what you believe. It may also work if one of you doesn't mind switching to the other's philosophy on money. Either way, my piece of advice in love and all aspects of life is to be eager to learn and to look for more information. Always be committed to constant growth.

FIRST IMPRESSIONS

Another thing that is so important with writing your love story is increasing your eye contact. Most people have no idea how important eye contact is early on in the love process. Of course it is important throughout any relationship, but this is a skill you must master to the best of your ability.

When you are talking to someone and you lock gazes with them, it can drastically increase the amount of emotion they feel because of chemicals produced in the brain. If you are single, you should practice this with anyone and everyone you come in contact with. Some people feel uncomfortable looking someone in the eyes as they speak, but it can drastically change the course of a conversation. Locking gazes can cause them to feel like you are totally into them.

In a world that is filled with a million things to distract us and steal our attention, here you are totally into this person. Not looking down every few words to check your cell phone. Not people watching at the restaurant. Not looking away every other word as if their face was repulsive. I mean looking them dead in their eyes as if each word was like a log in the game of Frogger for Atari. Each log and each word was just one step closer to staying alive. It is a great habit to intensely pay attention to someone when he or she speaks.

First impressions are everything, so if you come off to your new partner, friends, or even business associates as a complainer, then you will be known as the complainer. If you come across as a passionate and purpose-driven person, then that is how you will be perceived. First impressions can make or break your love story before it even begins.

Make no mistake about it. We live in a visual world. When you walk through the grocery store, that guy/girl doesn't look down the aisle at you and say, "Damn, girl. Check out his/her personality." It literally takes seconds for someone to decide if you could be a potential mate for him or her.

When preparing for a date with someone you have already been out with once before, you may still spend a lot of time getting ready for that date. You take the time to make sure your hair, nails, makeup, and perfume are perfect. Men make sure that their hair is well groomed, cologne is sprayed in the right places, and their outfit is just right.

I'm not suggesting that you shouldn't focus on these things when going out on a date. What I am suggesting is that you have already made the first impression (and, yes, if they see your profile picture on social media, your first impression has already been made.) So be sure you are confident with the pictures you have posted.

Chances are you have already made the first impression without actually speaking to them. You should focus on these things when you are single, but it continues even when you are in a relationship. Consider every day with your mate as a chance to make another first impression. You should look your best all the time not just when you are going out on a date.

I have had clients argue this point and say things such as, "They should accept you no matter how you look." Another thing I heard someone say is, "Trevor, are you saying that we as women can't look good unless we have makeup and heels on?" These are all very good points, but each digresses from the original point.

It's always interesting to hear someone indirectly share what is in his or her blueprint. Somehow she heard something that I never even stated (or believe for that matter). It is clear that she automatically assumed that she had accurately assessed me. Any more assumptions and she will make an ass out of herself. Maybe deep down in her search engine is "All men think we women have to walk around with heels and makeup on every day." Of course that is not what I said at all.

The point is, you determine what is your best. You can have sweatpants on and still look your best. I'm not talking about society's vision of what you should or shouldn't look like. Think of it this way. Pretend you are twenty years into the future, and you have been married now for fifteen years. Congratulations!

Now when your husband or wife is telling someone the story of how you met, wouldn't it be cool for them to describe you as the most amazing sight they ever saw? Of course you want them to think that way of you no matter how you look. I'm merely suggesting do your best to write that in the script.

WHY NOT BLOW THEM AWAY?

So the next time you are running to the supermarket, make sure you look incredible. Or if you have to make a quick run to the bank, be sure that your appearance is breathtaking. One thing is certain. If you meet the love of your life today, and you look less than your best, you can't take that back. You never get a second chance to make a first impression, so nail it every time. Even if you don't find your true love today, it wasn't a waste of your time, and it was not a failure.

Why?

When you leave your house and you look amazing, it should be for you more than for them. If you go through the day and you don't meet your mate, you may have a tendency to feel like you failed or that no one found you attractive enough to approach you. Eliminate that thought from your mind right now.

Primarily you should look your best as a sign of cherishing yourself. I would never suggest you primarily be your best for someone else, especially if you haven't met them yet. You should value yourself that much. In a way you are telling the universe to send you a person who also values you equally as much. You want to be on top of your game because you admire how beautiful and fine you really are inside and out.

Just like the man with his dream car, all he wants to do is hand wash it and treat it like it's his most prized possession. He covers it at night, because he doesn't want leaves falling on it or any other elements. You are your dream car. You could have an old coffee stain on your shirt. Maybe you rushed out of the house without brushing your hair. Maybe you have a hole in your dress. There are so many scenarios that could push away your potential partner.

LET'S GET READY TO RUMBLE

In addition to being physically ready for the first impression, you must also be psychologically ready. On the Discovery Channel, I watched a hunter take down a huge deer. The thing that stood out to me the most was that the hunter watched for hours through the scope of his gun. He was mentally and physically ready so that, when the deer appeared, the hunter's response would be a reflex reaction.

He was able to be himself, because he had practiced so many times that this kill was routine for him. When the deer emerged from behind the trees, the hunter was ready seconds after spotting it. This is where you want to be when your deer emerges from the next aisle in the supermarket or holds the door for you at the local office building.

When a man says, "Hello," that is not the time to say to yourself, "Okay, girl, make sure you smile." You should be smiling beforehand. Ladies, don't be afraid to wink at him. What do you have to lose? You should practice your people skills on everyone so that it is natural to respond to that handsome guy with a quick response of "Hello. How are you enjoying this beautiful Saturday?"

See how quickly that happened?

You immediately acknowledged him for speaking and also turned it back on him to respond with an answer of his own. Fellas, when she smiles at you in the pasta aisle, that is not the time to try to think, I wonder what I should say? How about you say hello?

Keep in mind that you have no idea when your ideal mate will come into your life, so just be prepared to dance with them in conversation. This is why being kind to everyone plays a role in how a relationship will be. I remember hearing a very interesting quote from T. Harv Eker. "How you do anything is how you do everything." You should work on being the best you can in any area of your life, because it could have an impact on every area of your life.

We all have a story, or blueprint, on what love SHOULD BE. This is why it is important to define what ideal love looks like to you, so you can identify whether entering into a relationship with someone will either be harmonious or fraught with a lot of conflict.

I always tell women, if you believe deep in your heart that you shouldn't have to approach a man, then don't. If you go against the blueprint or deep belief you have had probably most of your life, you may win the guy but end up with resentment toward him. This resentment is the result of feeling like you compromised the story you believe in.

Women also have to understand that some men are scared out of their mind to approach you. I know traditionally we are supposed to wrestle lions and hunt bears, but the fear of rejection is sometimes worse than death.

I think back to a client of mine whose desire was to become her best so she can attract a great mate. I told her, before she could attract a mate, she had to clearly identify what she was looking for and what she wanted out of love.

Shortly after she had created her blueprint, she found herself in a situation where she saw a guy who she was attracted to on a train. They both exchanged glances. Instead of letting the opportunity pass her by and end at one glance, she decided to get up, change her seat, and sit right next to the guy who had sparked her interest.

I love how she was able to make it a little easier for this particular guy. In fact most women often make the first move, with a brief smile, a blush, playing with their hair, etc.

When I asked this particular woman how she would have felt if he didn't respond to her bold move, she quickly replied.

"It wouldn't have shifted my mood at all. I would have moved on with life. The fact that I was confident enough to take the risk exemplified my growth as a woman. I wouldn't have felt rejection because I didn't really approach him. My only thought was in increasing the opportunity. I had nothing to lose by listening to the voice that said, 'Sit next to him.' I had everything to gain."

Her response blew me away. Far too often we allow someone's response to dictate who we are. Two big lessons that my client experienced during this encounter were to stay true to herself and to follow her gut. It's important to always be ready to receive your desires (in this case an ideal mate), as if it is already on its way. You can change your life, your blueprint, or both to find true happiness.

How many times in life do the right people cross each other's path for a brief moment that could spark everything, and they miss it merely because they were both afraid of rejection or just weren't thinking fast enough?

Another thing you want to do is have a balance of open-ended questions to keep the conversation going. Sometimes people are intimidated and afraid to make a move. Our society has painted a picture of superconfident men who should have no fear when approaching a woman. In reality, some men have been rejected by women who were almost as amazing as you are. This makes them second-guess saying something to you, and, by the time they decide they should say something to you, the chance to meet the perfect woman for them has expired.

However, if you gave those same people a little hint of your interest, you could watch their whole energy change in front of your eyes. So by keeping the conversation going, it is almost like getting a quick look at a person's life, at his or her personality. Remember they are doing the same thing to you, so you want to make sure that you show confidence and enthusiasm.

I'm not suggesting you put on a front for them. You should actually get to the point where you are confident and enthusiastic about life. You would be surprised how many women complain about not having enough quality men to choose from. Yet all it takes is for some woman to simply respond to that guy with a brisk "Hello." He threw you the perfect assist to show you that he was interested, and then you gave him nothing in return. Again you need to be like the hunter, always ready.

Men and women alike tend to want to be around people who make us feel valued. We want to feel amazing about ourselves when we are with you. The people around you love you because they know who you are. This is your first chance to let someone know who you are.

You should aim to do something slightly out of the norm for your first date. It may be in your best interest to get the adrenaline flowing so those feelings of exhilaration are associated with you. It could be going to the shooting range, riding roller coasters, watching a scary movie, etc. Stirring up someone's emotions can be a good thing. I'm sure you want someone who is emotionally connected to you somehow. Most people like to enjoy dinner, a movie, and many other common options on their first date.

Additionally many marriages have come out of these first dates so choose a memory-worthy activity. You want to avoid your first date being an interview session over a meal, though it will be impossible to avoid asking any questions at all. If you do ask questions about feelings, make sure they are open-ended questions. When you ask closed-ended questions, you stop the conversation dead in its tracks. When they can respond with a yes or no, you know that you are asking the wrong questions.

Asking questions about feelings is common for women, who are sometimes considered feeling beings. When you ask well-placed questions about how a man feels, it allows you to get a glimpse into what he values. You get a first-class window into his blueprint. Either way, have fun and remember you are creating the fairy tale.

Sooner than later, you want to find similarities between you and your potential spouse. Once you notice them, you want to highlight them. For some people, it already seems difficult to find someone who doesn't drive them crazy. Never mind someone who is just like them. When you highlight the things you have in common, you get a chance to create or live in their ideal or blueprint. At the same token you need to pay attention to the things that you don't have in common.

Let's take Charles for example.

Charles called me because he was extremely confused on which woman to choose. He was dating Tasha and Angela, and was ready to select one of them to commit to. So how did he make the decision, you ask?

Although they both seemed to be perfect potential mates, only one could take on the role of partner. Tasha didn't have children, and she had initially expressed concern about Charles having a child. It was clear that her blueprint showed she wanted to be with a man who didn't have to deal with his baby's mother.

She later claimed that she was willing to accept his situation, but her original feelings were already out there. It also wasn't very easy for her to let go of the fact that he had a child.

This made Charles's decision fairly easy because Angela already had a daughter and was more than accepting of a mate who already had a child. There would be no need to convince her, because she could relate to him being a parent.

Can you see how paying attention to a person's actions and conversation can allow you a window into their blueprint?

Now back to the all-important first date. One of my female clients went on a first date with a guy, and they were having a great time. After their meal was done, the waiter handed the check to the guy. She immediately snatched the check and said, "I'll pay for it."

He then insisted that he didn't feel right, as a man, letting her pay for the first date. Her response was, "Don't get caught up in those gender roles." She smiled at him thinking he would be impressed. She then gave her card to the server, and that was the end of it.

She called me a few days later to explain how the date went, and she told me that he didn't call her back for a second date. When I heard about the exchange over the check, I smiled. Here it is a strong, independent woman who didn't know how to turn it off.

He had clearly let her know his definition of a man, which doesn't allow her to pay for the first date. He was almost screaming, "Here is my blueprint. Here is my ideal." He told her what his ideal was for the first date. She heard his plea, but didn't recognize being the independent woman in this instance was trampling on his manhood. No wonder he didn't call her the next day.

You have to pay attention to people because they subconsciously tell you how to love them. It's not always with words. Sometimes they do it with gestures. They show a blush here or a smile there.

The worst thing to do is spend years with someone who can't meet your needs and you can't meet his or hers either. It's paramount to have a partner who loves you the way you need to be loved. Some people have great sex and never take the time to evaluate if their potential partner is in the running for their heart. If you don't have a plan, then any road will lead you there.

Sometimes your future spouse may want or need certain things in order for his or her to feel satisfied in a relationship. Identify your partner's wants and needs that you naturally meet. While doing this, you should also identify your partner's wants and needs that don't come as easily to you.

Look also at how your partner is able, or not, to meet your own needs. If what you truly need becomes a burden for him or her, you may have the wrong partner. Loving someone doesn't have to be hard if you find the right person.

Your partner shouldn't change who he or she is for you. That would cause that person to go against years of training. Now if it's something he or she wants to change or doesn't mind changing or won't resent you for later, that's great. For the most part, you will get in the future whatever you see consistently now. There is no point in marrying someone based on his or her future potential if you don't see evidence of it in your partner's life currently.

Of course you can learn a great deal from conversing with your potential partner, but often it is more important to pay attention to their actions. Sometimes people will tell you one thing, but their subconscious involuntary responses reveal exactly who they are.

It could be as simple as a blush or a smile to let you know that you have struck something in them by your words or actions. Often people show a flash of anger toward a subject, and they have no idea they have just given you a glimpse into what drives them crazy.

You have to decide if you want this person and if you can meet this person's needs. It would be wise to try to understand what it is like to be that person by entering his or her world. Finding love really is like being offered a box of chocolates, because experience and knowledge teach you how to choose what you want. Sometimes you never know who a person is on the inside until you try them. Oftentimes you may have to go through exactly what you don't want to get what you do want.

I'm sure you remember that time you thought you had chosen the best chocolate until you bit into it and said, "Damn! Wrong one!" Sometimes it's just a game of numbers. Experience teaches you to identify the ones you probably won't like or, in this case, it will identify who will not be the best partner for you in the long term.

UNDERSTANDING YOUR TARGET

Most of us spend so much time trying to be understood. If you talk to someone about themselves, they will listen all day. This is usually the case with men but is not limited to just guys. Most people will reveal who they are in their language. When I speak of language, it doesn't always have to be verbal. A large part of communication comes from someone's tone of voice and his or her body language. I facilitate workshops where we spend at least an hour going over what different physical gestures could mean.

You can often learn someone's fears, wants, needs, insecurities, and goals just from his or her language. Most people realize the importance of sincere flattery but oftentimes make the mistake of complimenting their potential love on something he or she is already confident about. If you want to set yourself apart from the noise of every other voice, it would be wise to tailor your flattery to their insecurities.

If a woman is very attractive and she recognizes this, complimenting her on her beauty may fall on deaf ears. If this same woman is insecure about her teeth, a subtle compliment on how perfect her smile is could make her feel more valuable. Those words could enhance her worth, and she could associate that feeling with you.

Most men love to be complimented on the size of their penis. However, if a guy already knows that he is well-above average, telling him he is big below the belt may do nothing new for him. If this same guy has a height complex, complimenting him on how he is the perfect height for you will more than likely increase his confidence.

Make sure your compliments are genuine of course. I'm a huge advocate of being yourself if you want to find your ideal mate. It is very hard to live a lie. Finding love already takes some work. Why make it more difficult by not being your true authentic self?

Treat your potential partner as someone special, make it hard for them to see anyone else. Once you are used to filet mignon, it is very difficult to go back to Hamburger Helper.

Find someone who has natural qualities that attract you. These qualities will stir up your emotions. You will have more energy. You will be more animated, and you will have more creativity. These are all skills every screenwriter of the blueprint of life possesses.

Let's face it, we all have insecurities. How cool would it be to find someone who loves you exactly the way you are?

So when choosing the right person for you, it is important to find someone who responds to you in a way that shows you love. If you are short, you probably want

152

someone who isn't obsessed with a tall spouse. If you are very thin, it is probably best to find a potential spouse who appreciates a thin lover. It is best to find someone who loves you the way you are, not for what you could be. I can't stress enough how important finding the right partner is.

People are looking for adventure and pleasure. When we were children, we had no restrictions and very few cares in the world. Bring your partner back to that place where he or she doesn't have to be judged for his or her actions. The world has stripped us of fun and given us responsibilities instead. Make life a fantasy, a fun ride into forever.

Take a second to ask and then answer this question: What is seductive about you? Use whatever answer you come up with as a basis to make your role in your love story a starring role.

CHAPTER SUMMARY

- You have more control over your love life than you think. Stop leaving things to chance. Discover some of the things you have control over.

- Always be physically and psychologically ready for a person or situation that could change your life.

- How do you measure up to your potential partner regarding your major values? Is there balance when it comes to what you both bring to the table?

- You never get a second chance to make a first impression so make it a great one.

- See the world through your potential partner's eyes and try to understand his or her psychology. Learn what that person's blueprint is and decide if it is something that matches yours.

THE 60/40 AXIOM

PRINCIPLE OF LOGIC AND EMOTION

An important thing to keep in mind during the dating process is that things or people will not change when you get into a relationship.

The person who is in front of you is exactly who you will be in a relationship or marriage with. I believe it is very important to give people a chance to show you who they are. This means no pressure until you are sure this person makes sense for you emotionally (40 percent) and logically (60 percent). What this means is to spend more time evaluating if they make sense for you logically. How you feel is important, but remember feelings often change.

Ideally you want to know that person's goals and have an idea of what his or her blueprint is for life and love. However, if you are dating a lazy man, then you have a lazy boyfriend presently or a lazy potential husband in your future.

If the woman you are dating is very confrontational now, it is safe to assume she will be confronting you more than a few times in your relationship.

Think about when someone gets a document notarized. They take it to a person who will make it an "official" document. At some point the final step is affixing a seal or stamping it to acknowledge it is notarized. Even with a stamp and witnesses, the content of the document never changed. The only thing that has physically changed is the stamp that was applied.

It is best to consider dating in the same manner. Consider "getting married" as the stamp placed on the document. The document is your relationship. Nothing changes once you are married. You will just get more of the same person you have been getting.

Love the person for who they are right now. If you find yourself falling for their potential, you may be limiting your decision to those chemicals the brain produces. Remember, there is no reason to make a permanent decision based on a temporary emotion.

You have to have the confidence that you are bringing the best "you" to the table. This purpose for sharing my story is so that you can find inspiration in it to become better a "you" and to find your own story. You must have the confidence to move on if someone isn't right for you.

There is not a shortage of good men. You might as well get rid of that thought now. There isn't a shortage of great women. Please just let that thought go. Your ideal partner is waiting for you to be found, but again you have to be ready when they cross your path.

"Trevor, I just realized I messed up."

These are words from a friend of mine. For the past few weeks I have been coaching/counseling her on success principles, and how they apply to dating effectively and having a great relationship. For some reason our session the other day hit her hard, and she had an *aha* moment.

It has been about two years since she had dumped this guy who she swore wasn't right for her. At the time, I told her that her thoughts were the cause of her problems. I urged her to hear me out, but she felt she did not need to listen to my advice, or "dating lecture," as she called it.

Recently she finally allowed me to guide her through the dating process. I talked about a chapter in my book that touches on how we all make up stories that seem so real sometimes that we believe it. After about thirty minutes into the call, she started to cry. At that moment she realized it wasn't her ex-boyfriend's fault; it was her all along. Unfortunately he had already moved on.

One day I was at my aunt's house, and she offered to give me some of her favorite flowers from her garden. She went outside and cut a few peonies. She told me that these flowers are so strong that, if you put a few in any room, it will smell as if you are burning several candles. She also warned me that, if I didn't decide to take them at that time, I would have to wait until the following summer for them, since they only grow in that four-week period.

As I sat in my car that day, it hit me. We all have peonies in our life. It could be Mr. or Mrs. Right or an opportunity to earn more money. If a YEAR represented a LIFETIME; there are some things that we would have to wait another lifetime for, to take advantage of, if we didn't seize the moment while it was here. The most important thing is to be ready to pick them.

My aunt made sure I took advantage of these lovely flowers so I wouldn't have to wait another year to experience them. I realize some people may pass up their ideal spouse and may have to wait for another lifetime before they get an opportunity to find someone so special.

This is why I focus so heavily on the 60/40 principle and how to apply it to finding your ideal spouse. This basically means that selecting your ideal partner for marriage should be based on 60 percent logic and 40 percent emotion. If you haven't noticed already, I have given you the 60/40 principle throughout this book.

When looking for your ideal spouse, it is important to embrace the emotions and allow yourself to get swept up in the whirlwind. However, it is more important to let your personal logic guide you beyond how you feel. I say "personal logic" because most of the principles discussed in this book are designed for you to specifically apply them to your life. You and I have gone through different experiences so we may see the world differently.

There is no exact cookie-cutter way to finding your success with love. There isn't another you in the universe. You are one of a kind. Think about it. No one in this world has your fingerprints. Out of all those millions of sperm, only one made it to fertilize that egg. You are supposed to be here now. Just think, no one in the world has been around you every moment of your life but you. You were there when you cried in the car, and no one else was around. You were there when you took that piece of candy, and you knew it was wrong. No one else shares your exact story.

Here is the dating world through my eyes. Once I learned the principles described in this book, I applied them to my life, which allowed me to find the perfect woman for me. Navigating through the dating scene was a fun experience because I now knew what to do. I also expected to find my ideal wife one day, so there was no need to put pressure on myself to expedite the process. You have to remember that you control your thoughts, which directly affect your life and results.

After Tracy and I broke up, and I moved out, I was able to find the perfect bachelor pad. One of the first things that changed my life was no longer watching television. I knew that, if I was going to become great, I would have to stop letting in the outside influences from the media, aka the secondhand TV smoke. This was not one of the sources of information which I wanted my self-talk to pull from.

I lived in that apartment for an entire year without a television. I also started to create my own commercials. All over my house I had printed multiple copies of my affirmation statement and put them on my walls. Every room in my apartment was a constant reminder of what I wanted. My affirmation statement was about my life in general, but there was one line in there about a future love. "I now have an amazing wife that treats me like a king." No wonder I would eventually find such a woman.

In the mornings, when I exercised, I would do incantations with certain parts of my affirmation statement. I'm sure my neighbors thought I was crazy as they would see me jogging down the street talking to myself.

Through unending studying, I've resolved that there are core parts in everyone's blueprint. These core ideas (that I dive into detail below) seem to be the most common desires for men and women.

WHAT DO WE GENERALLY NEED?

We all desire an attractive spouse, men and women alike.

I have heard on many occasions that men are visual, and as a man I can confirm this. Many publications will tell you that a man needs an attractive wife. I knew the woman who could stop me dead in my tracks would be a woman who was absolutely breathtaking.

Also I knew that I had to look my best in order to attract that type of woman. I knew that I wanted a woman who felt the need to always look good for herself, which of course I liked too. I wanted her confident in herself, but I needed a woman who wanted to strive to always impress me physically. Not only because she was emotionally driven by me but because she understood how important that was to me.

Ironically one day I heard Zaida mention someone on TV making a comment about not having to look good for her man because she had already "got him." Zaida was very annoyed with this woman. She couldn't understand why a woman would actually lower her physical standards after she became married to her husband.

Her disgust for this woman's mentality gave me a peek into what my future would be like if I was with Zaida. Remember, I wanted to see those involuntary responses to get a glimpse into how she really felt. I saw a woman who would present her best self even at sixty years old and not just now in her early thirties.

Affection is another crucial part of a relationship. I knew that any woman who I came across was going to have a strong desire for affection since it was a need for most women. Showing affection wasn't that difficult for me.

I had spent so many years with Tracy trying to express affection in so many ways to no avail, that it was now easy for me. In the past I had thought that, if I had showed her affection, Tracy would actually start to develop feelings for me. It's funny how we may see something as a failure, but it is really preparing us for a great life.

I also learned something that most guys always get confused about. Affection is not sex. For most men we see sex as a form of affection, but, through coaching, I have helped many men expand their expressions of sex to include affection to meet the needs of their woman.

There is no secret that men and women need and want sex. I wanted a woman who physically desired me and whose sex drive equaled my own. I realized how important this was because, after five years of being unhappy sexually, I knew that would not be the environment I wanted for my future wife or me to be in for the next thirty or more years.

I also knew that for sex to be something enjoyable for most women, there would have to be an emotional connection often fueled by affection.

Most women have an inherent need for conversation. I had learned this years ago, but recently being in the car with my wife really drove this point home.

Zaida and I were on our way to the train station early one morning. I clearly remember driving and having a conversation in my head about what I had to do for the day. I knew I would have to check my email as soon as I got a chance. I also knew I would have to post my latest thought on social media. There were at least three people who I needed to speak to right away regarding my workshop.

While I was having this conversation in my head, Zaida said something. It was like a radio station not quite on the right channel. I could hear bits and pieces of what she was saying, but I was still preoccupied with my own conversation.

Finally I decided to turn my radio frequency to her channel, and I discovered she was doing the exact same thing that I was doing. She was literally mapping out her day, step by step. Instead, she was doing it out loud.

It was at that moment I truly understood a woman's need for conversation. She didn't need my manly opinion. She didn't desire my expertise. She simply just wanted to talk. There have been plenty of times when she came to me with a question, and it was apparent that she didn't want an answer from me.

How often do women go to men with a challenge, and the first thing a man wants to do is solve the problem?

In most cases, women really don't want or need our opinion. They just simply want to talk. I knew that, in order to truly please a woman, I would have to master the art of listening as part of having a conversation to the best of my ability. Women shouldn't have to apologize for wanting to converse. Men should just learn more about how to accommodate.

By now you can tell from my story that I had a strong desire to be praised by my woman. Being praised was a form of admiration for me. For me, pride was a big deal.

Oftentimes men get in trouble with another woman because the other woman puts them in such high regard. They go home, and their wives are pointing out all the things wrong with them. Meanwhile, their mistress doesn't see them as often, so they may be unaware of their men's flaws.

I knew that the woman I would marry wouldn't allow any other woman to outperform her when it came to building me up, admiring me and respecting me. I had a vision of walking out of the house every day ready and willing to take on the world. I wanted my woman to understand this was important to me specifically.

Most women desire commitment. To pledge your love to her, and only her, has been a desire of hers since she first watched *Beauty and the Beast* when she was a little girl. Of course, a woman must really like you in order for this to be true. It isn't like any guy can have any woman by giving his love exclusively. There needs to be some sort of attraction to him first.

Along with that commitment, she has a strong need for complete honesty. Nothing hurts a woman more than finding out something from someone else that she should have heard from you.

Recreational support is another big need in a relationship since men love to recreate in different ways. After interviewing over one hundred married/divorced couples, I noticed a common trend among the women who had been married ten years or more: learning to love the things that are fun for him.

One woman told me that her husband loves to go bowling. In fact she understood this so much that she even purchased herself a ball and made sure she was with him every Tuesday night at the bowling alley. She eventually got to the point that she loved it just as much as him.

Now I'm not suggesting you become obsessed with something that doesn't interest you. What I am saying is to find a way to at least enjoy something that he does.

If he loves football, you can't be the only one in his life telling him how much time he wastes watching it on Sundays. If you really don't understand it, show interest by asking questions. I don't mean interrupt him after every play but show him that you want football time to be a time you both can enjoy.

Of course you are both individuals and will have different interests but you should each make the attempt. If he likes going to the gym, you might as well get your workout bag out of the closet and join him. Maybe he'll be game to try yoga with you next time.

Through my years of research, I've identified that some traditions are traditions because they work. In the past the man was charged with the duty of going out and hunting. It was the man's job to provide for his family. As a matter of fact women would choose a man based on his physical stature. A man's body would tell how good of a hunter he was, which would equate to how much he could provide.

Armed with this knowledge I knew that I wanted to be with a woman who deserved my efforts to take care of her financially. I remember hearing a pastor say, "It isn't that a woman doesn't want to work. It's just that deep down most women don't want to have to work."

In today's society women work just as hard and long as men do. As a man, I believe you should put your woman in a position where she can work if she chooses to but doesn't need to. Obviously this means that men should be chasing after their passion and building their income long before they get married.

KNOWING AND DOING ARE TWO DIFFERENT THINGS

As discussed in *Lights, Camera, Action*, you are the writer, director, and main actor in the role that is your life. While "auditioning" women for the role of my future wife, I used the concepts of logic and emotion to determine if each woman was right for the role. These a just a few real-life experiences that I will present to you as case studies to show my thought process when dealing with logic and emotion. Being able to accurately define the balance between the two ultimately led me to finding my amazing wife, Zaida.

ROCHELLE

I met a woman named Rochelle through a mutual friend. She lived about three hours away from me in another state. Every other weekend I would head down to D.C. to see her. We had a lot in common. We both loved good food and trying out "new" restaurants. Most of our dates consisted of one person introducing the other to a different type of cuisine.

We also had an unusual connection when it came to humor. We would spend 90 percent of our time laughing.

She made it easy to have a good time wherever we were. These were things that were important to me. We had a natural chemistry, and I enjoyed our time together.

After two months I started to realize that the distance was an issue. I also realized that she didn't seem nurturing, like a mother or wife. She was more of a best friend than an ideal spouse for me, based on our interactions, limited by distance. I had already spent five years with a best friend. I needed more.

Although I was dating other women closer to me, I just couldn't imagine having to drive three hours just to get some. Yeah, I said it. There was no way I was going to move to her state, and she seemed pretty established where she lived. Of course we would have made it work if the emotions were strong enough, but they weren't.

I loved being around her, but overall she didn't affect me to the point that my creativity was in full force. However, where my logic finally came into play was on New Year's Eve. I drove down there to hang out with one of my best friends because a few of us were planning to go to a huge party in the area.

I knew she would be going to another party, but it was fine because we had planned to meet up after the festivities. We were texting most of the night, and I couldn't wait to see her. As I started to head to the hotel where she was staying, I got terribly lost. I tried to call her several times to get better directions, but she wouldn't answer her phone. I figured that she'd had too much to drink and couldn't answer her phone. I finally had to use my phone's GPS to find the hotel.

I finally found her hotel and asked the front desk what room she was staying in. Once I got to her room, I knocked on the door. I heard a lot of movement but no one came to the door. After about five minutes of feeling like I was being played, I went back downstairs to the front desk and requested that they call her room. When the guy at the front desk called her room, he said that a guy told him to tell me to go away.

I went back to my hotel by myself. I wasn't angry or upset. The next morning a few of us went to eat breakfast at this amazing restaurant in the city. On my way to the buffet line, guess who I saw? Yep, you got it. And she was with some other guy. Of course I didn't say anything because it didn't make sense to ruin what was probably an incredible New Year for her.

Here is what my logic screamed to me. If she was drunk the night before, she would surely see my text the next morning while eating brunch, right? If she really wanted you, Trevor, she would have been fighting to contact you the next morning, right, Trevor?

You can see the type of energy my blueprint was made of. I wanted to make sure that love and respect and passion created by those brain chemicals we discussed in the True Love section were in abundance. I never got a text that morning. If I was that important, she would surely contact me and apologize for standing me up. Later that day, I told her that I saw her at brunch, and it was cool.

Needless to say, I was now clear that she wasn't my ideal woman. And my interest in her rapidly declined. She later told me that the guy who told me to "go away" was a good friend of hers. She claimed that she didn't do anything with him, and he was just taking care of her since she was so out of it the night before.

The thing about knowing what to look for in an ideal spouse is that you don't need their explanations. Her actions already spoke so loud that I couldn't hear what she was saying. Dating is more about seeing if their blueprint matches yours. Only you can determine that. I didn't want a life filled with events like this.

KEISHA

I had met Keisha years ago at my after-school job in high school. It had been a long time since I had seen her, so to bump into her as an adult was refreshing. She was unapologetically attractive and very career driven. She made it clear that she wanted a family in the future, and I could tell she would make a great mother. We would grab a meal together often, and her personality was addictive. Her eyes and her smile captivated most men.

One day over dinner we started talking about sex. She knew about my last relationship where I simply wasn't getting any. She told me about her past relationship, where sex was something she enjoyed and initiated often. Of course I was excited because, at that time, it seemed like sex between us was going to be magical.

That was when she said something that changed our connection forever. She told me that she "would not be having sex again until she was in a committed relationship." She was making an admirable choice. I respected her for holding her ground on such a special interaction. From that point on, I started pulling back from her romantically. We would still hang out often, but one day she told me that she had noticed the difference, and that it was like night and day.

I wasn't doing it on purpose but, after she had brought it to my attention, I started to see what she was talking about. My logic took over. For me to get into a relationship with someone without knowing if we were sexually compatible would be love suicide.

I'm not saying that this should be everyone's approach, but again I spent five years unhappy sexually, and I knew my choice had to be a little selfish when it came to my needs. Sure I could get it anywhere, but I needed to know that my next relationship would be my last. I just wasn't willing to get into a relationship just to find out there were no fireworks in the bedroom.

The other thing that didn't sit right with me logically was the fact that she had had sex with others in the past and didn't require a relationship from them. Why did she allow sex to ensue with those other guys before a relationship? It was as if she had no control. There must have been something about them that made her just give in. And now that we were dating, she has all this control.

Can you see how my knowledge and experiences helped shape my blueprint?

I wanted a woman who wanted me as bad as I wanted her. So much so that she had to act on it. I did love that she had such strong values, but, remember, I wanted someone that I affected to the point that it stirred something in them that they couldn't explain. I wanted her emotions to cause her to move slightly out of character.

Yes, I wanted my ideal woman to lust over me in addition to all the other positive feelings. I would only be mad at myself if we eventually got married and had challenges in bed. I saw the computer lab with Tracy all over again.

If Keisha had so much control now over sex with me, surely she could hold out on me when she is angry ten years from now. I know we are speaking of sex here, but you can replace that word. I knew how prepared I was to meet the right woman's needs. To hear that there were already conditions on my number one need was a huge disappointment.

I know some people may feel I was reading too much into it, and my self-talk was out of control, but let me say this to you now. Most people won't change as time goes on, and you have to choose a spouse based on who they are now, not who they can be.

Of course she had probably set this new requirement based on her failure with love in the past. So actually she, like me, was using her personal logic to guide her to her ideal man.

The man who really wanted her would wait until there was a relationship. Needless to say, we eventually stopped talking to each other, but she is now engaged to a man who agreed to abstain from sex until marriage. Both Keisha and I had things we weren't going to compromise, and it worked out for the best.

MIRIUM

I ran into Mirium at the mall one day after doing a presentation. It had been years since I'd seen her. We had never dated in the past, but it was clear that we were completely attracted to each other. She was dating a guy who wasn't giving her all the attention she felt she deserved. This didn't help the fact that she was very insecure about the way she looked.

This lack of confidence in herself was very unattractive, but it didn't completely turn me off. What really pushed me away was when she described to me what her ideal man looked like: six foot two or above. If you have never met me before, I clock in at a whopping five nine.

She also noted a few other qualities that her ideal man would possess. She told me, indirectly, that I wasn't the ideal man for her. At that moment I figured she couldn't possibly think we would be together in the future. We hung out all the time because she was truly a good friend of mine.

Months later, when I told her that I had found the perfect woman for me, she began to flip out. I couldn't imagine why she was so upset with me because we never had conversations about being together.

I even invited her on at least two dates that she had declined, so I truly felt she wasn't interested, which caused me to lose interest in any potential relationship with her. I had heard Tracy mention in the past how she liked tall men, so I would not allow myself to force someone to change their type and make an exception for me.

Remember, anyone can find a partner, but very few even know how to find their ideal partner. Since I was the director of my love story, I didn't feel like I had to force someone into the role. If Mirium hadn't been so passionate about her description about her ideal man, I may not have thought much about it. I just didn't want any wife of mine to feel like she was settling for less.

TISHA

Tisha was a few years older than me and already had two children. She explained to me that she'd had challenges with her last pregnancy and didn't want to have any more children. I didn't have any children yet, so of course that wasn't music to my ears.

When we started dating, I told her that we couldn't work out because of that issue. She agreed, but our connection was so strong that she said she would possibly have another child for me in the future. Although I was truly flattered and blown away by that statement, I knew it wouldn't work for me.

If she had a child *for me* and didn't want one, it would only be a matter of time before she resented me. Of course this wasn't guaranteed, but there was a stronger chance of it happening. I didn't want her to change her core beliefs, wants, and desires for me. Not regarding something as important as children.

What her statement did tell me is that I had a strong impact on her. Of course I truly wanted that from my prospective wife. I also knew that I needed my relationship to make sense for her as well as me. So we agreed to enjoy the time we had with each other, but I know she wasn't happy when I finally came to her and told her I had found my potential wife.

It was a bittersweet moment at the time, but obviously it worked out for me. It is women like Tisha who inspired me to write this book. There are so many great women like her who will come alive if they can just find the right guy to inspire them too. That guy will also make sense logically as well.

ZAIDA

Zaida and I went to the same college, made up of over forty thousand students, and, for some reason, we would run into each other fairly often. We never connected romantically in college because she had a man and I had a girlfriend at the time. It's funny how things work out. I would see her updates on social media but never really thought much about pursuing her. After all I was living the single life and loving it.

One day I decided to reach out to her to see where she was in life. One of the first things I noticed was that she was being a little distant. After conversing with her, I realized she thought I still had a girlfriend. After she learned that I was actually single and not some player, the conversation started to move in the right direction. Although I was all about dating pretty women who were into me, I couldn't help but respect the fact that she was concerned that I was with another woman exclusively.

I was impressed right away. Here is why knowing everything I know was essential to my success in dating. I was ready to hang out with her, but it just so happened that her birthday was coming up in a few days. She informed me that she already had plans for the weekend, so I would have to wait until the following week to take her out on a date.

For me that was fine, because I had someone else who wanted to go out with me anyway. So even if I wanted to be thirsty, I couldn't be, because I wasn't betting all my money on any one person yet. Some people fail just because they don't have enough bets or they simply don't have enough horses in the race. I knew that, since it was around her birthday, I would have to do something a little special. Sometimes God sets it up perfect for you, and you have to be ready with your bold move. If not, you miss the opportunity to create a fairy tale.

I thought she had to be dating at least one other guy, and I wondered what he was going to do for her birthday. I was competing with a guy I had never met. So instead of waiting until the following weekend, I wanted to hang with her while her birthday was still fresh on her mind.

Here is the amazing part of the story. Zaida later told me that she had been through so much with love and relationships that she had started to feel like she was horrible at choosing the right guy. She also told me that the night before I actually contacted her, she had prayed to God and had basically told God that choosing the man for her was in HIS hands. To her surprise I contacted her the next day. Wow, talk about a love story in the making.

I told her on Friday to keep her Monday open so we could go out on a date. I told her it would be a surprise and that she would have to trust me. You have to think, if this person you are dating ends up being your spouse, what memories will you look back on? One thing is for sure; today is the memory of tomorrow, so make it count.

I knew our first date would have to be something where the adrenaline was flowing. I had no intention yet of making her my wife. Hell, I had no intention of making her my girlfriend even. I knew she had potential just based on appearance and personality, but that was it.

I had recently been to the shooting range by myself, and I thought it was an incredible experience. I thought that would be a great place to take a potential wife on a first date. My assumption was that most women have not been to a gun range, and they would be slightly scared or nervous. I would stand out as the confident man who would gently guide her through this potentially dangerous process. I knew that I couldn't take her to dinner or a movie because she has had other guys do that over the years.

I did not let her know where we were going until we pulled up to our destination. Of course she was shocked that I had planned a date at the shooting range. When we have conversations about how we met and how we arrived at the point we are at now, it's always an interesting story.

When it was time to load the weapon, I made sure I stood close to her. I wanted her to feel safe. I constantly encouraged her. I wanted to make sure that I established a love connection between us. I had a romantic dinner set up for later, and, yes, I stole my first kiss.

I made constant eye contact with her throughout the night, because again first impressions are everything. I wanted her to feel like it was all about her when she was with me. Sure, I had done this in the past, but the circumstances surrounding our particular date were prime.

It was her birthday week; she had always wanted to go to the range; she had just prayed for God to send her the right man. I could have easily missed my chance if I wasn't ready to pounce on the opportunities in front of me.

I certainly didn't stop dating other women because no one would occupy all of my time unless I knew without a shadow of doubt that we were right for each other. One day she came by my apartment, and, in a joking manner, she asked, "Did you clean up all the bobby pins?"

With a big grin on my face, I responded, "Yep, I think I got them all."

I didn't feel the need to hide this from her. I loved that she joked about it. This was one of the things I respected about her. She didn't feel the need to investigate too much into what I was doing with my free time. If she was the type of woman to demand a monogamous relationship too early, she would have scared me off. She gave me my space while we enjoyed each other's company.

I knew I didn't want a needy woman, but, at the same time, she needed to show me the type of attention that let me know she was completely into me. I spent time explaining my blueprint. She later told me that she had a time frame in her mind for when she needed me to start talking about a committed relationship.

We never made it to that deadline, even though I was never made aware of it beforehand. This meant that at least a part of her blueprint was met. She obviously expected a guy to know that he wanted to be with her, after giving the time, energy, and money she was giving to our long-distance relationship.

Zaida lived about 1.5 hours away from me, so, when either of us came to see the other, it was a fairly big deal. Some weeks I would actually make the sacrifice to drive to her twice in one week. She would do the same.

Years later I heard her mention that she had dated guys who had complained about the commute to come see her, and they had only lived thirty minutes away. Here I was making that three-hour-long round trip journey to see her with no hesitation.

The fact that she stirred something in me that made me want to drive to see her said a lot about her. So it was clear that my emotions were there. She also admired my willingness to shorten the time frame between visits despite the hassle of New York traffic.

By now, the other women I was dating just didn't seem to compare. Most of them never mentioned children or didn't even really express a desire to have them. I would always hear Zaida talking about her nieces and nephews, and how she loved them so much. This was a clear indication of how much she loved kids and how great of a mother she would be. I needed a little more than her words though.

In addition to things she would say, I would see pictures of her changing diapers when she was a child herself. There were plenty of pictures displaying her love for children in her family. Then I would see how great she was when all of her nieces were with her. She truly came alive when children were around. Of course there is no true way to tell how great of a mother she would be, but it was clear that she had experience with raising children.

As a man I loved that she kept her house clean and occasionally she would wash my dishes at my apartment. She wasn't auditioning. You could tell this was just the way she was. She wanted to take care of a home. Somewhere in her life, she had decided that is what a great woman does. She was still the strong, driven, independent woman. All of her behaviors were in line with what I thought my prospective wife's should be. Our blueprints were in sync.

We had many discussions about our family and different memories we had from childhood. One of the things we shared in common was that both of our families loved to travel. There were places in the world I had never dreamed of going to that she had visited. There were plenty of destinations that I had seen that she was still anxious to see.

So one day she mentioned going to visit her old friends in the Bahamas. Of course I immediately thought how wonderful that would be to hang out with her on the island. I could only imagine how much stronger our bond would be after a trip like that.

With no hesitation at all we decided it would be cool to go away for a few days. So here it was three months into dating, and we were already hanging out on a beach resort together. If this wasn't laying down the perfect foundation for a fairy tale, I don't know what was. Our time on the island was magical.

Remember how I told you the story about the yellow brick road in the chapter on True Love?

Remember how we talked about choosing what you want to think and believe in the chapter entitled What Were You Thinking?

Some people don't realize how important the journey is until you discover who you are.

Back when I was a sophomore in college, I remember traveling with my family and my current girlfriend to Mexico. I wanted to find something to do. Unfortunately I was the only one who knew how to swim, so, as a group, we had very few options. After reading through the brochures, I noticed there was an opportunity to go snorkeling in the ocean. I didn't think it was a big deal at all.

I thought they would just give you the goggles so that you could see underwater. I knew they would also give us the tube to breathe through, so we could observe the beautiful fish and plant life.

Look, I'm from a place called Newark, New Jersey. Snorkeling was not a subject that was discussed often while I was growing up. I would see pictures of people floating on top of the water and looking at the beautiful environment.

I thought that all you had to do was walk off the beach and go into the ocean with the equipment. This would allow you to choose how deep you wanted to be. I figured, how bad could this be? Since my sister and girlfriend at the time couldn't swim, I thought this was a safe bet. I talked them into going snorkeling with me, and, to my surprise, they agreed. This was truly going to be exciting.

When it was time to meet the group participating in this activity, we were required to get into a very small boat. There were about ten of us, including the captain of the small vessel. I figured we were getting in the boat just so that we could go to a different part of the beach, and this way would be quicker.

After about two minutes, we were cruising along the shore, but we were getting farther and farther away from it. By this time I started to panic without showing it on my face. I couldn't imagine why we would be three miles away from the safe sand.

The boat was so small that I could easily dip my hand into the water. The boat stopped. "Okay, everyone out," the captain said. I looked over the side of the boat and all I could see were huge black figures that I couldn't identify.

I imagined sharks swimming all around us. While I'm thinking these thoughts, all of the other passengers willingly jump overboard. Of course my two ladies were looking at me as if to say, "Well, you got us out here. So what are we going to do?" I had to make a decision right there on the spot. Either I was going to fight through my fear of the unknown and lead the people who were very important to me, or I would let the fear stop me from following through.

So with great hesitancy, I slowly got into the water. I didn't want to take them this far and waste all the money our family had spent for us to do it.

First thing I did was look down in the water with my goggles. The water wasn't as deep as I thought it would be. Sure, it was about fifteen feet before you reach the bottom, but I could actually see the bottom.

For the remainder of our time in the water, we all gradually started to get the hang of it and had an awesome time. Right when I started to feel confident, the captain yells out, "Look to the left of the boat. You will see a barracuda." I don't know about you, but a barracuda sounds like a huge sharklike animal.

Here I am panicking inside all over again. Overall, it was an amazing experience because no one I knew at the time had done it before. I was proud that I was thrown into such an unfamiliar environment. It forced me to grow quickly.

Fast forward ten years and I'm in the Bahamas with Zaida. I figured going snorkeling would be amazing. It was something that could get the adrenaline flowing just like it did at the gun range on our first date. What's interesting is she had gone snorkeling in the past with her family, but she had refused to get off the boat. I didn't learn this until years later, so imagine the love story being created. Here we are doing something she was once afraid to do, but I was the one to assist her in facing that fear.

If I hadn't convinced my sister and a former girlfriend to go snorkeling back then, I probably would have stayed on the boat as well. Now here was my opportunity to expose her to something that no other guy had. The difference in the Bahamas was there would be no other snorkelers on the boat. This time around it was just Zaida, the captain, and me.

I didn't have the comfort of knowing that other people were in the water with me. I can't explain to you how beautiful the fish and ocean were that day. We also had bread on the boat, and, when you take it into the water with you, the fish surround you just trying to get a piece. They don't bite. I guess they are more curious as to why you are way out here in their territory. There were at least one thousand fish swimming around us when we broke the bread up into little pieces. It was the perfect adventure.

Three months after our Bahamas trip, Zaida was scheduled to go to Jamaica with about fifteen other friends. They had booked their trip a year in advance. I had such a great time with Zaida in the Bahamas that I didn't want to miss the opportunity to be in paradise with her again so quickly. Since I had the extra money, I decided that I would book the trip. It was the perfect opportunity to write my love story as I saw fit.

A few days after I had booked my accommodations, I realized that one of my best friends would be getting married the same weekend. This was a huge dilemma for me because I truly wanted to be there for him on his big day. However, I understood the incredible value of being able to travel with Zaida twice in six months. I already had a strong feeling that she could be the woman I would marry. Being with her in such a beautiful place again was the ultimate form of isolation. There are no cell phones, just adventure, sun, and beauty.

I felt that my friend had already found the woman he wanted to spend the rest of his life with, and I was still writing my story. For this reason, I decided not to cancel my travel accommodations. Sure I could afford the airline penalty for canceling, but it wasn't about the money. It was more the fact that, if I missed this trip with Zaida, I may have missed an opportunity to solidify an incredible foundation for love.

Remember, we had just had an amazing time in the Bahamas. Why would I miss the opportunity to join her in doing something she loved, especially since I loved traveling as much as she did? I told my friend I wouldn't be attending his wedding. I was confident that Zaida would be mine after another trip. We were already together, but I wanted her to see her future when she saw me.

That was part of my blueprint.

I was of course one of the new guys, since this was my first time meeting some of Zaida's friends. Additionally, out of all of the romantic encounters we had had on that Bahamas trip, one of the most memorable events took place in the middle of the ocean.

It seemed fate had come full circle. More than half of us decided to go snorkeling. I knew that I wanted to repeat what Zaida and I did in the Bahamas. I envisioned going out in the water and hanging with Zaida. The only difference was that her friends would be in the water with us.

Eleven of us boarded a medium-size boat and went fairly deep into the ocean. That is when I realized that only about four out of the eleven had snorkeled before. I don't remember the order, but I do remember some people getting into the water and jumping right back out as if to say, "What the hell am I doing way out here?"

For the most part everyone enjoyed themselves, but only half of us stayed in the water. I helped one of Zaida's friends, Angie, to get the hang of it by making sure she was comfortable with her equipment. After a few minutes, she appeared to be a pro. She acknowledged that she was more than fine on her own.

I ducked my head underwater and began to swim the forty feet back to where my future wife was floating. I must admit the wind was very heavy this day, so, if you stood still in the water, the current would push you a few feet away from where you were originally. I was exhausted by the time I finally caught up to her.

Zaida and I started to remove our goggles so that we could speak to each other. Suddenly she looked behind me as if she'd just seen a unicorn. She yelled out, "What happened to Angie?" I turned around. When I finally saw Angie, I could see her arms moving and water splashing. It appeared as if Angie was drowning. "Go save Angie," Zaida shouted.

I put my head underwater and started swimming as fast as I could. As I approached Angie, the driver of our boat jumped into the water with all his clothes on. We both got to her around the same time, so we helped her get into the boat.

After a few minutes she was absolutely fine, but she was no longer interested in snorkeling that day. I finally returned to Zaida, and we enjoyed our time in the water. When we all got back on the boat, I remember everyone talking about how great the day was.

They began talking about Angie, but I was shocked that they were so excited about my efforts to save her. I believe they were impressed with the fact that I was swimming as fast as I could to save someone I had just met one day prior. Another young lady even made a *Baywatch* reference. I felt appreciated by all of Zaida's friends at that moment.

Later that day I started to give that event a meaning. To be honest, Zaida probably already knew that she wanted to spend the rest of her life with me before this trip. However, I still felt there had to be some effect on a woman when she witnessed her guy working hard to save her friend when she told him to. If I would do that for her friend, what would I do for her?

This opportunity to demonstrate why she could feel comfortable in my arms had presented itself, and I was able to act on it. How many opportunities have passed you by because you weren't ready? We write our love story every day, every hour, every minute, and every second.

CHAPTER SUMMARY

- Embrace how you feel for that special person but make sure he or she match the person you are.

- Understand your needs and the needs of the person you are with.

- Understanding what you want allows you to pass up on seemingly once-in-a-lifetime opportunities that aren't a fit to your blueprint.

- It makes logical sense to disassociate with anyone who doesn't match your blueprint.

- Your past heartbreaks and failures contained a blessing and a lesson. Take the time to look back and understand how everything you have been through can help you become everything you want to be.

- You have the ability to blow your special someone away with your actions as long as you play close attention to what has an effect on him or her.

SETTLING IS NOT OKAY

TYING IT ALL TOGETHER

I've shared a lot with you throughout this book. However, one of the most profound lessons I've learned is that you must go beyond your challenges and give love.

Everything you want is outside of your comfort zone. You have to be in a position to receive all the good that wants to come into your world, and that cannot happen if you do not feel and give love.

Feelings of anger, frustration, worry and despair are all feelings that block your blessings. Once you learn that all human beings are connected, you will see the world in a new light. Sometimes you meet someone who is drastically different from you. Just understand that their life experience can be diametrically opposed to yours; which may account for all of the differences the two of you may have.

When you are looking at that thirty-year-old guy, you are looking at thirty years of history. Thirty years is equal to approximately 15,778,500 minutes. It took that much time to make that man. My best advice for someone looking to find and keep their ideal partner would be to follow the 60/40 principle of logic versus emotion.

While the emotion is an important factor, there is a reason why logic is weighted much heavier in the equation at 60 percent. Logically take a moment to evaluate if this person matches who you are and your core values.

In addition to taking time to truly evaluate a partner, it is equally important that you spend some time really getting to know yourself. Take the time to create your blueprint and analyze why you are the way you are. After analyzing, spend more time making sure you bring the best version of you to the table.

At the end of the day your goal is to home in on your logic; pay close attention to see if this person makes sense for you long-term. Don't get so caught up in right now that you overlook the red flags that can and will surface tomorrow. You should embrace your feelings to evaluate if this person can cause the type of emotions you want to experience in love.

The final step in carrying a new relationship to the altar and beyond is to constantly look for more information, books, seminars, etc., to improve yourself. A relationship that has two people committed to meeting each other's needs and learning how to do better each day can create miracles.

Remember that timing and your ability to be prepared is everything.

When I met my future wife in college, she had a boyfriend. That wasn't the right time. I had to learn some things, and so did she. We both had been hurt by love and had to learn things about ourselves. It is so difficult to truly appreciate a sunny day if it never rains. If you ask my wife, she will tell you the same thing.

No one can make you happy but you; NO ONE!

Don't put pressure on someone else to make you happy. Projecting your vision on them isn't fair to them. Accept them for who they are right now, and, if you don't like who they show themselves to be, just move on. Remember, if you feel it will be hard to find the right person, that is exactly what you will attract in your life. Prince Charming is not going to change your thoughts for the most part. However, you have complete control, so get in the habit of happiness now.

Learning how to conquer obstacles (within yourself and within a relationship) are mission critical for maintaining the fairy tale you are in charge of creating.

As I type these last few words, my wife and I are expecting our first child. What most people didn't know is that we were originally expecting twins. We had already received two or three different ultrasounds from separate doctor visits showing us our two babies. One day during our routine visit, we received a different doctor for that particular day.

As we watched the monitor, excited to see how much the twins had grown, the doctor made a comment that would alter our days here on out drastically. He began to tell us what will happen to the baby whose heart had stopped beating.

"Excuse me," I yelled at the doctor. Apparently it was written in our file during our last visit that only one of the babies still had a heartbeat. No one decided to tell us. To add insult to injury, the doctor insisted that we might have heard what we wanted to hear and not what was actually said.

We were insulted. I may be getting older, but I think I would remember hearing that we would no longer be having twins because there was now only one fetal heartbeat. If there was only one heartbeat at our last visit, why did that doctor give us a printout of the ultrasound showing two babies? I find it hard to believe that a doctor would give us a picture of two babies with two arrows pointing to both hearts if there was only one heartbeat.

All I could think about was what my wife could possibly be feeling. I can't imagine what a woman thinks or feels when losing a child. Sure, the baby wasn't born yet, but we still had a connection to our unborn children. The rest of the day seemed to move in slow motion.

I kept hearing my father's advice for life. "If you don't like something, you should change it. If you can't change it, there is absolutely no reason to stress over it."

This wasn't just my motto for this situation; this was my motto for my life. After all, there was nothing I could do to bring back the child who was now gone. I instantly began to focus on the blessing that was still in my wife's stomach. Any energy expended—being angry with a doctor, God, or each other—would be stolen energy that should be going to loving our son.

Ironically, when I reached out to Zaida, it was clear that she was also focusing on the blessing. It just didn't make sense to focus on what we had lost without appreciating what we had gained. Who knows? Maybe God's purpose for our son was so big that He could no longer allow him to share the womb.

I look at an event like this and I realize, more than ever, how important it is to find your ideal mate. Who knows how this situation would have been handled if we were not on the same page?

You have to decide right now that settling is not an option. You have to be willing to wait as long as it takes to find the person who allows the two of you to share a symbiotic relationship. Once you find that person, there will be no wave big enough to cause your hands to separate. However, in order to get there and stay there, you can't be afraid to take off your shoes and work for it. Of course it is much harder to walk on sand because the ground is morphing with every step.

So, yes. . . . There will be challenges along your path, but just keep this in mind. The only way to enjoy the cool refreshing ocean called "happily ever after" is to be willing to walk through the sand, hand in hand, and get your clothes a little dirty together.

NOTE FROM THE AUTHOR

Through his 60/40 principle of logic versus emotion, he lays out the blueprint on how to attract, identify and keep one's ideal partner. As shared in *Never Settle*, "Anyone can find a spouse, but very few find their ideal mate. Finding is reserved for the searcher. However, the search is only successful if you know how to look. *"Never Settle*, shows you how to look.

Known as the "Dating Designer" Trevor's goal is to help you design your personal plan to find and keep "Mr. or Mrs." Right. By living the phrase "actions speak louder than words," his skills, research and life experiences were utilized when choosing his life partner. As he has done with countless others, Trevor shares in his book how he used the same skills to navigate the complex dating scene to finding a valuable partner; which ultimately led him to marrying his amazing wife!

ABOUT THE AUTHOR

Trevor Andrew Scott is no stranger to helping others. As an influential dating and relationship coach, he has an unrivaled ability to connect with a diverse scope of individuals.

Before helping others find their ideal partner, he began his career as an insurance broker. Throughout his tenure, he led hundreds of personal development trainings and empowered over 10,000 individuals to achieve more by becoming more.

While building his brand in the insurance industry, Trevor experienced a devastating setback when a 5 year relationship came to a disastrous halt 2 months prior to his wedding day. Following the relationship's arduous demise, he was determined to show himself and others the difference between knowing a path and actually walking a path to living an exceptional life. Sharing his experiences with others became his ultimate purpose. His mission was to help others find the right partner so they can build a solid foundation for a lasting relationship.

Trevor realized that choosing the wrong spouse has a direct impact on how one succeeds in life. Choosing incorrectly hinders productivity because so much energy is spent on fixing the relationship instead of the relationship being complementary to one's success. A successful relationship is something people can attract by the person they consciously become. Additionally, having such success can be taught. As he began to document his realizations, he deepened his scholastic research interning with an accredited marriage counselor and subsequently obtained a coaching certification.

Beyond the Book

Connect with Trevor

Trevor is so committed to helping you find and keep your ideal partner that he has created several workshops and sessions where you can continue the conversation beyond the book and focus on your unique needs.

60/40 Workshops: The "60/40" Workshops also known as "Boot Camps" are specifically designed to challenge your belief system because you cannot live beyond your belief system. Your life is what you think it should be. So if you want to change your life, you have to change your thinking. Thinking changes by what you believe. The workshop sessions will help you discover the best "you" possible.

Personal Coaching Sessions: Since no two people are the same, all personal coaching sessions will be tailored to you specifically. Sessions will serve as a place for you to practice the habits that will make you successful in finding and keeping love. Your instinct will become more equipped to make the right decisions because Trevor will help you mentally prepare in practice to be ready to make better decisions.

Speaking Engagements: Trevor is available to host or serve as an event panelist and moderator.

To register for a session or for more information regarding booking go to **www.trevortreoscott.com**. Once you have registered, special instructions will be sent to you on how to receive special discounts on personal coaching sessions and workshops.

Made in the USA
Middletown, DE
30 January 2015